## Pains of Youth

...nd Bruckner (Theodor ...
an Austrian playwright who established his reputation
with *Krankheit der Jugend* (*Pains of Youth*, 1926) and
...her (*The Criminals*, 1928). Subsequent
...cluded *Elisabeth von England* (1930) and
...pretation of Shakespeare's *Timon of Athens*
...) as a criticism of Nazi Germany. Bruckner wrote
...e persecution of the Jews in *Die Rassen* (*The
... efore emigrating to the United States
... Hitler's seizure of power. *Die Rassen* became one
of the most successful plays of German exile theatre.
He returned to Germany in 1951, where he became
dramaturg at the Schiller Theater. His last plays were
existentialist tragedies in the classical tradition.

Martin Crimp was born in 1956. His plays include
*Definitely the Bahamas* (1987), *Dealing with Clair*
(1988), *Play with Repeats* (1989), *No One Sees the
Video* (1990), *Getting Attention* (1991), *The Treatment*
(winner of the 1993 John Whiting Award), *Attempts on
Her Life* (1997), *The Country* (2000), *Face to the Wall*
(2002), *Cruel and Tender* (2004), *Fewer Emergencies*
(2005) and *The City* (2008). He has a longstanding
relationship with London's Royal Court Theatre, and
more recently with the Vienna Festival and the Festival
d'Automne in Paris, which commissioned his first text for
music, *Into the Little Hill* (2006), written for composer
George Benjamin. He has also translated works by
Ionesco, Koltès, Genet, Marivaux, Molière and Chekhov.

# FERDINAND BRUCKNER

# Pains of Youth

## (*Krankheit der Jugend*)

*in a version by*
## MARTIN CRIMP

*faber and faber*

*Kra...* ...                                                           1926

This English version © Martin Crimp 2009

The right of Martin Crimp to be identified as author
of this work has been asserted in accordance with Section 77
of the Copyright, Designs and Patent Act 1988

A CIP record for this book
is available from the British Library

ISBN 978-0-571-25564-1

2 4 6 8 10 9 7 5 3 1

**Pains of Youth** was first presented in the Cottesloe auditorium of the National Theatre, London, on 21 October 2009, with the following cast:

**Petrell**  Leo Bill
**Lucy**  Sian Clifford
**Marie**  Laura Elphinstone
**Irene**  Cara Horgan
**Alt**  Jonah Russell
**Freder**  Geoffrey Streatfeild
**Desiree**  Lydia Wilson

*Director*  Katie Mitchell
*Set Designer*  Vicki Mortimer
*Costume Designer*  John Bright
*Lighting Designer*  Jon Clark
*Music*  Paul Clark
*Music for Extended Piano*  Simon Allen
*Sound Designer*  Gareth Fry
*Movement Director*  Kate Flatt
*Assistant Director*  Caroline Leslie

# Characters

**Marie**

**Desiree**

**Irene**

**Freder**

**Petrell**

**Alt**

**Lucy**

The girls are all very young, the men a little older

*Place:* Vienna

*Time:* early 1920s

PASSAU (the Bavarian village) is stressed on the first syllable, and the second syllable rhymes with 'cow'.

## Passages in square brackets

[*thus*] supply the sense of incomplete or ambiguous lines. These passages are not part of the spoken text, nor are they alternative readings.

## Notes

All notes, including footnotes, have been added by MC.

## Thanks

My thanks to Laura Gribble for preparing a literal translation and generously answering my many questions about the German text. Thanks also to Gerhard Willert of the Landestheater, Linz.

# Translator's Notes

## The text

This translation is based on the text published in 1928 by S. Fischer Verlag. Bruckner subsequently wrote an alternative ending to the play which can be found on page 114 of this edition.

## The title

This edition retains the play's traditional English title. It should be noted however that the original title, *Krankheit der Jugend*, means 'the illness/disease of youth/of being a young person'. Bruckner thus joins his contemporaries in extending the concept of 'disease' to society at large – a potent twentieth-century metaphor which could at one extreme underpin political ideology, while at the other inspire the humane literary genius of fellow writers Thomas Mann (*The Magic Mountain*, 1924) and Sigmund Freud (*Civilisation and Its Discontents*, 1929).

## Pronunciation

DESIREE is pronounced 'deziRAY' and stressed on the last syllable, like 'disarray'.

IRENE has three syllables and the same stress and vowel sounds as 'retainer'.

FREDER rhymes with 'trader'.

PETRELL is stressed on the second syllable.

# PAINS OF YOUTH

*The action takes place in Marie's room,
in a boarding house.*

# Act One

## SCENE ONE

**Marie** (*at the door to the lobby*) I need you *now*, Lucy.

**Lucy** (*off*) Coming.

**Marie** And with hot water.

*Lucy enters with bucket.*

**Lucy** You're doing cleaning?

**Marie** (*already scrubbing the floor, laughs*) Friday's my big celebration.

**Lucy** Big celebration for what?

**Marie** (*laughs*) I graduate. I'll be a fully-fledged doctor.

*Bell rings, off.*

**Lucy** Room four wants their breakfast. (*She goes.*)

**Marie** (*works, then after a pause*) Dizzy? Are you still in bed?

**Desiree** (*from her room*) I'm having a wash.

**Marie** (*again at the door to the lobby*) Clean water for the windows. And a duster.

**Lucy** (*off*) I'm coming.

## SCENE TWO

*Desiree appears from the adjoining room.*

**Marie** Up already?

3

**Desiree**  Test me. Behold the hideous volume.

**Marie**  When's your exam?

**Desiree**  Ten.

**Marie**  (*keeps scrubbing*) Fire away.

**Desiree**  The Lung. (*Yawns, stretches.*) This is so ridiculously early.

**Marie**  Are you scared?

**Desiree**  Scared? I'm not even awake yet. Right. 'Advanced tuberculosis with cavitation. Tuberculosis with cavitation does not differ in principle from common tuberculosis because the formation of cavities is only a secondary effect of necrosis.' (*Laughs, puts her legs up on the table.*) Our darling Irene's made a bet she'll qualify before I do even though she's a whole year behind.

**Marie**  (*still busy*) Where are the cavities formed?

**Desiree**  'At the places where the illness first occurred, in the superior lobes and subapical areas.' Revolting creature.

**Marie**  Ambitious – but she's beautiful.

**Desiree**  Red-haired little reptile. She'll go far.

**Marie**  Smaller cavities.

**Desiree**  'Smaller cavities may occur in the relatively early stages of the illness.' Freder's after the maid.

**Marie**  (*surprised*) Lucy?

**Desiree**  I caught him sneaking out of her room.

**Marie**  Bastard.

*Desiree laughs.*

**Marie**  So that's why she's had that haunted look.

**Desiree**  And started to limp.

**Marie**  (*laughs*) Started to limp?

**Desiree**  Yes, when a woman's out of her depth with a man it changes the way she walks.

**Marie**  Rubbish.

**Desiree**  Anxiety. Depression.

**Marie**  (*cautiously*) And what about you?

**Desiree**  Oh – me – I was over him ages ago.

**Marie**  But you were obsessed with each other.

**Desiree**  (*laughs*) Used to be. He was the first man I ever saw the point of. It felt good with him – really good – right down to my fingertips. He's not just powerful – he's a virtuoso. But even with a virtuoso it gets boring in the end.

**Marie**  (*straightforward*) You have to love the man – or you'll always end up bored.

**Desiree**  Is that what you've got with your friend Dolly: love? – love all soft and innocent?

**Marie**  (*laughs*) He's not so innocent, thank you very much.

**Desiree**  (*surprised*) Oh really? I assumed he'd have no idea what a woman needs.

**Marie**  (*smiles*) And what does a woman need?

**Desiree**  (*goes up to her*) Only a woman knows what a woman needs. (*Tenderly.*) Marion. I'm going to call you Marion – like my sister. Those were my most blissful moments – when the governess said goodnight to us, switched off the light, and went. I'd crawl straight away into Marion's bed – and we'd lie there – pressed close together – we'd kiss and each of us would feel the warmth of the other's body and know what it was. Life – it was the warmth of life. Which I've never felt again – not since I was a child.

**Marie** (*extricates herself*) Come on – I'm not Marion.

**Desiree** Why can't we go on being children all our lives?

*She hugs Marie again.*

Then you wouldn't be Marie, you'd be my sweet little Marion.

**Marie** You're not really asking to be a child again.

**Desiree** I want the warmth – I want to be all wrapped up in cotton wool.

**Marie** Well I don't. I want to be me – now.

*She gets back to work.*

**Desiree** Is all that scrubbing really necessary?

**Marie** I want to celebrate in a clean and decent room. You only qualify once. No more being a student. From now on things get serious.

**Desiree** Clichés. Don't kid yourself.

**Marie** It's not clichés, it's my life.


### SCENE THREE

*Lucy.*

**Lucy** I can help now.

**Marie** Clean water for the windows and the mirror, please.

*Lucy goes off with the bucket.*

**Desiree** (*laughs*) The rivals exchange glances.

**Marie** Leave her alone.

**Desiree** Didn't you notice the look?

*Lucy brings in the bucket of clean water.*

**Lucy** Clean water.

**Marie** Thank you, sweetheart.

**Desiree** Is Herr Freder coming today?

*Lucy looks at her, startled, and keeps silent.*

It's just a question.

**Marie** Getting nice and clean in here, don't you think?

**Lucy** (*dully*) Yes.

**Desiree** You're a pretty girl.

*Lucy stares at her, surprised.*

**Marie** Take a good look round, Lucy – everything's going to totally sparkle.

**Desiree** I'm serious. You have very pretty eyes.

**Marie** The one thing I've still not got is music.

**Desiree** A person could really fall in love with you.

**Marie** It won't be a celebration if I've not got any music.

**Lucy** (*quickly*) The gentleman in room nine's away. He's got a gramophone. I'll go and get it.

**Marie** You're an angel.

*Lucy goes.*

**Desiree** (*calling after her*) Chin up, Lucy. I'm a friend. Poor bitch.

**Marie** (*now working on the mirror*) On we go. How about larger cavities?

**Desiree** 'Larger cavities worsen the prognosis since they tend to collect pus.' Notice the limp?

**Marie** Symptoms?

**Desiree** 'Symptoms of cavities – which hardly ever occur simultaneously – may include: 1. On Percussion, (a) Tympanitic Resonance, (b) Metallic Chink.' *

**Marie** When do you get the Metallic Chink?

**Desiree** 'When a large superficial cavity opens into a bronchus.'

**Marie** That's brilliant.

*Desiree yawns.*

You're so gifted it's like an illness. The fun's meant to be actually having to work.

**Desiree** I wish I could run away from lectures the way I ran away from home when I was seventeen. I wish Daddy could sit there all strict in lectures with the horsewhip out while poor sweet hopeless Mummy cries because I'm bad but fastens her pearl necklace all the same and goes off to the ball. I wish I could have all that back again. Only childhood's worth living.

**Marie** I wouldn't want my childhood back. My parents hated each other.

**Desiree** So did mine. But the thing is, Marion, when you're little, even that's fun. It's only later you start to

* 'Percussion' is tapping of the chest and back to listen for different sounds which aid diagnosis; (a) and (b) are examples of such sounds.

realise [*how terrible life is*]. Everyone should shoot themselves at seventeen.

*Marie laughs.*

After that it's just more disappointments. Which I thought I could run away from. With silk stockings, no money, and a very thin coat.

*Pause. In the meantime Marie has begun altering a dress.*

Studying, cleaning, dressmaking, boyfriends – what's the point? Why make so much work for yourself?

**Marie** What you call pointless, I call beautiful. That's the difference.


### SCENE FOUR

*Lucy with a letter.*

**Lucy** A gentleman. He's waiting outside.

**Desiree** Did you follow what I said, Lucy? You're very pretty. Don't undersell yourself.

**Marie** (*glancing through letter*) Quick. I don't want Dolly meeting him.

*She goes off with Lucy. Desiree grabs the letter, looks at it, goes into her room, returns with money – banknotes – and quickly stuffs them into the envelope.*

(*Coming happily back in.*) That's him got rid of. I've bought Dolly a rococo writing-table. He said that with an antique writing-table he could do much more beautiful writing – you know – stimulate him –

**Desiree** (*bursts out laughing*) You're such an idiot.

9

*Marie is about to throw away the envelope, notices the money. She looks at Desiree, surprised.*

**Marie**  Was this you?

**Desiree**  (*jumps up and hugs her*) Little Marion.

**Marie**  I can't accept it.

**Desiree**  Such an idiot. (*Kisses her.*) What [*are you so surprised about*]? Because you're in love with a man. I have to take care of you.

**Marie**  You're totally mad.

**Desiree**  We're both of us mad – because I'm in love too – only with you.

**Marie**  Let go of me.

**Desiree**  (*kisses her passionately*) Only women know how to help each other.

**Marie**  Let me go.

**Desiree**  (*with a wild laugh*) No, I won't let you go. No, I won't. Not unless you / promise me – [*you'll think about my love*].

*Marie pushes her away. Pause.*

**Marie**  We're not talking about it any more.

**Desiree**  (*pale*) Marion.

**Marie**  You're being stupid. (*She sits and starts sewing again.*) Right. Symptoms on percussion: '(b) Metallic Chink.' What's (c)?

*Desiree looks at her and heads for the door.*

The money, Dizzy.

*Desiree takes the money and her book. Goes into her room. Marie watches her leave. Pause. Goes to the door.*

You should be ashamed of yourself – silly baby. (*Tries to open the door.*) Open the door. I didn't mean to hurt you. Open the door, Dizzy.


### SCENE FIVE

*Freder.*

**Marie** (*tense*) What?

**Freder** I need to see Dizzy. The other door's locked.

**Marie** So's this one.

**Freder** Oh?

**Marie** It's none of your business.

*Freder watches her.*

(*Tense.*) I've never found your presence very welcome. I believe in frankness, Herr Freder.

*She folds up the dress.*

**Freder** The graduation dress. Am I right?

*Marie is silent.*

Congratulations.

*Marie is silent.*

You've achieved more in five years than I have in twelve. 'Fine specimen of a woman' I believe is the phrase. Just like I'm a fine specimen of a man.

*Marie looks at him. Freder holds her gaze and laughs.*

**Marie** (*with contempt*) Shame you've no brain.

    *Freder laughs.*

You should get a job in a freak-show.

    *Freder laughs more intensely.*

Or why not try hanging yourself?

**Freder** You'll come running sooner or later.

**Marie** You're already drunk.

**Freder** So?

**Marie** Shame you've no brain.

**Freder** I'm not someone to be ignored. Ask Dizzy.

**Marie** She despises you.

**Freder** (*friendly*) Not in bed, my angel.

**Marie** How dare you.

**Freder** Just you watch darling Irene move in on Dolly-boy.

**Marie** Irene?

**Freder** Sterile little bitch.

**Marie** You're not to call Herr Petrell 'Dolly'.

**Freder** I genuinely like him.

**Marie** Nobody cares [*who you like*].

**Freder** Sweet – but totally ineffectual. Oh, he gets women aroused . . . in an erotic-maternal kind of a way.

**Marie** Have you quite finished?

**Freder** I am entirely non-judgemental. (*Takes a bottle of brandy out of his pocket.*) Congratulations.

**Marie** (*tense*) That wasn't necessary.

**Freder** You're pleased really.

**Marie** You're wrong.

**Freder** Fully-fledged doctor.

**Marie** I don't want presents.

**Freder** Don't want presents from me.

*Marie is silent.*

I'm inviting myself.

**Marie** The party is private.

**Freder** Even better.

**Marie** You're extremely intrusive.

**Freder** And you – young lady – are extremely rude.

**Marie** Maybe.

**Freder** Why is it you can't stand me?

**Marie** You're right. [*I can't.*]

**Freder** It's really quite dangerous –

*Marie laughs.*

Yes, dangerous to hate another human being quite so much.

**Marie** I don't hate you.

**Freder** Let's just see what happens, shall we?

**Marie** You've got a very high opinion of yourself.

**Freder** (*laughs*) And rightly so.

## SCENE SIX

*Desiree wearing a hat.*

**Marie** (*quickly*) I'll come down to the university with you.

*She puts her hat on. Desiree smiles at Freder.*

**Freder** (*laughs*) Her ladyship has an exam?

**Desiree** You look much better today.

**Freder** Give me your hand [*to kiss*].

**Marie** I'll take your jacket.

**Desiree** He already stinks of alcohol.

**Freder** You left me.

**Desiree** Consolation [*i.e. Lucy*] was near at hand.

**Freder** I'm not asking to be consoled.

**Desiree** Don't you mourn for me a little?

**Freder** What man could forget you?

**Marie** (*impatient, to Freder*) So – are you coming as well?

**Desiree** (*laughs*) You must be joking.

*She hurries off, followed by Marie.*


## SCENE SEVEN

*Lucy.*

**Freder** (*calmly*) Lucy.

**Lucy** (*standing still*) I have to take the water out.

**Freder** What water?

**Lucy** (*point to the bucket*) Over there, Herr Freder.

**Freder** You're lying. (*He sits down, to one side.*) When people fetch buckets they don't creep about. Come closer. What d'you want?

**Lucy** (*afraid and helpless*) Herr Freder.

**Freder** Shall I tell you?

**Lucy** You're hurting me.

**Freder** Where? I'm not touching you.

   *Lucy is silent.*

Where am I hurting you?

   *Lucy tearful.*

When you saw the other two leaving you wanted a little moment alone with me – mmm?

**Lucy** (*softly*) Yes.

**Freder** It takes courage to get what you want. 'Take out the water' – that's a lie – because what / you really [*wanted*] –

**Lucy** You're hurting me.

**Freder** Where, for Christsake? I'm not even touching you.

   *Lucy slowly starts to cry.*

(*More gently.*) Hey hey – you're a good little baby.

**Lucy** (*looks at him in surprise and goes over*) Herr Freder.

**Freder** (*strokes her hair*) Good little baby.

*Draws her down to him and pats her back.*

You're my puppy dog.

**Lucy** Yes.

**Freder** My tame little animal.

**Lucy** Yes. Yes.

**Freder** (*lifts her head*) Let me see your eyes. (*Pause.*) Clear beautiful eyes.

**Lucy** (*softly*) Yes.

**Freder** (*kisses her eyes*) Has no one ever told you?

**Lucy** (*softly*) No.

**Freder** Did you get back to sleep last night?

*Lucy shakes her head.*

Why not?

**Lucy** (*smiles*) Herr Freder.

**Freder** (*runs hand through her hair*) D'you love me?

**Lucy** (*smiles*) Please don't [*ask that question*].

*Freder pulls her close to him.*

(*Submissive.*) Herr Freder.

**Freder** (*kisses her*) So young and lovely.

**Lucy** (*submissive*) Somebody might come in.

**Freder** I want you very much.

**Lucy** (*kisses his hand, nearly in tears*) Oh God.

**Freder** Say it.

**Lucy** I can't.

**Freder**  (*softly*) This morning?

    *Lucy nods.*

Say it.

**Lucy**  I can't.

**Freder**  Did you do it?

    *Lucy nods.*

What?

**Lucy**  Both rings.

**Freder**  Frau Schimmelbrot's.

    *Lucy nods.*

Did she stay asleep?

    *Lucy nods.*

You're sure she didn't notice?

**Lucy**  I'm sure.

**Freder**  Go on [*with the story*].

**Lucy**  I can't.

**Freder**  Where were the rings exactly?

**Lucy**  In the chest of drawers. Second drawer down.

**Freder**  You knew they were there?

**Lucy**  She always hides her jewellery there.

**Freder**  Did you use a candle?

**Lucy**  There was light coming in.

**Freder**  What light coming in?

**Lucy**  There's splits in the roller blind.

**Freder**  Did you go up to the bed first?

**Lucy**  Yes, like you said.

**Freder**  How close?

**Lucy**  Up to the bedside table.

**Freder**  What was on the bedside table?

**Lucy**  A glass of water and hairpins.

**Freder**  Frau Schimmelbrot's.

*Lucy nods.*

Hairpins like these? (*He loosens her hair.*)

**Lucy**  (*submissive*) Herr Freder.

**Freder**  (*kisses her hair*) Amazing smell.

**Lucy**  Somebody might come in.

**Freder**  Let me see your eyes. Beautiful eyes.

*He kisses her eyes.*

**Lucy**  Herr Freder.

**Freder**  Where are the rings?

**Lucy**  Under my pillow.

**Freder**  Someone might find them there.

**Lucy**  (*afraid*) Shall I go and get them?

**Freder**  Hide them in the dining room.

*Lucy nods.*

Under the sideboard.

*Lucy nods.*

Now get up.

*Lucy moves away from Freder.*

I'll come to your room again tonight.

**Lucy** (*almost a whisper*) Yes.

**Freder** We'll make love again.

**Lucy** Yes.

**Freder** What are the rings like?

**Lucy** I didn't look.

**Freder** Gold?

**Lucy** I don't know.

**Freder** Frau Schimmelbrot hasn't realised?

**Lucy** She's still asleep.

**Freder** What about when she realises?

**Lucy** She doesn't wear the rings much.

**Freder** She'll realise eventually.

**Lucy** (*unconcerned*) I've no idea [*what she'll do*]. (*Suddenly.*) No one 'll think it's you.

**Freder** What's it to do with me?

**Lucy** (*quickly*) Nothing – no one will find out about you – they'd have to kill me first.

**Freder** About me? What the hell d'you mean? You're the one wanted them.

**Lucy** I'm the one wanted them.

**Freder** It has nothing to do with me. Put your hair straight [*i.e. tidy*].

*Lucy does so.*

I want to help you.

**Lucy**  Herr Freder.

*Freder embraces her.*

(*Submissive.*) Somebody might come in.

**Freder**  Maybe Frau Schimmelbrot.

**Lucy**  Herr Freder.

**Freder**  Why 're you shaking?

**Lucy**  It's not me I'm worried about.

**Freder**  Weren't you taking the water out?

**Lucy**  What water?

**Freder**  (*points to the bucket*) Over there.

**Lucy**  (*doesn't move*) Yes.

**Freder**  Take it out.

**Lucy**  (*doesn't move*) Yes.

**Freder**  And the rings.

**Lucy**  (*wakes up*) Yes. Under the sideboard.

**Freder**  And don't make me grovel around for them.

**Lucy**  By the right leg under the carpet.

**Freder**  By the right leg under the carpet. Take the bucket with you.

*Lucy takes the bucket.*

Move.

**Lucy**  Herr Freder.

**Freder**  Is it too heavy?

**Lucy**  No.

**Freder**  Shall I help you?

**Lucy**  (*quickly*) No.

**Freder**  (*goes to Desiree's door*) I'm going for a lie-down.

**Lucy**  (*frightened*) Yes.

**Freder**  Not jealous, are you?

*Lucy is silent.*

Of Desiree? Just you remember: she's a countess.

**Lucy**  (*vehement*) Who ran away from home.

**Freder**  (*laughs*) Absolutely right.

**Lucy**  When she was seventeen she'd / already started –
[*going with men*]

**Freder**  How old are you then?

*Lucy is silent.*

So keep your mouth shut.

**Lucy**  Every night she's / in there with – [*some other man*].

**Freder**  Don't spill the water.

**Lucy**  I hate her. I'd rather / be a – [*servant than a shameless tart*].

**Freder**  Mouth.

**Lucy**  Herr Freder.

**Freder**  I'm going to lie down.

*Goes into Desiree's room.*

**Lucy**  (*softly*) Herr Freder.

## SCENE EIGHT

*Irene and Petrell.*

**Petrell** Nobody here?

**Lucy** The young lady's got an exam.

*She goes.*

**Irene** (*laughs*) Desiree and her exams.

**Petrell** (*stretches out*) Marie must've gone with her.

**Irene** Do make yourself at home – Dolly.

*Petrell laughs.*

Marie and her little Dolly.

**Petrell** Please will you stop now.

**Irene** Can't you take a joke?

**Petrell** It was bad enough out in the street [*being called Dolly*].

**Irene** Fine then, I'll stop. Anyway, everything she does is stupid and pointless.

**Petrell** Who?

**Irene** Desiree. She's a dabbler.

**Petrell** She still managed to catch up on school in just one year, when all she'd ever had at home was some idiot private tutor.

**Irene** Only because Alt spent every night cramming it into her.

**Petrell** And she's still getting distinctions in all her vivas.

**Irene** Because she's a countess. She's no idea about *work*.

**Petrell** Please calm down.

**Irene** You and me 've spent our whole lives clawing our way out from under – and *still* no one notices – *still* we're invisible. Even at university it's the egos like her who come out top, not the people who work.

**Petrell** Creative people can have egos too. [*He means himself.*]

   *Irene laughs.*

Don't stop [*laughing*]. It suits you.

**Irene** She's only one year ahead of me now. We'll see who qualifies first. Christ – I can't believe I actually *care*.

**Petrell** Please calm down.

**Irene** It's just play-acting. We all know what's really on her mind. I've got more time for a whore in the street – at least they're honest about what they get up to.

**Petrell** But you do still want to become a doctor?

**Irene** I'm not letting some spoilt brat aristocrat put me off. But it won't end happily: she'll end up like every other sad little slut – in an opium den.

**Petrell** (*laughs*) For godsake.

**Irene** Or the mortuary.

**Petrell** (*gets closer to her*) Why 're you always so bitter?

**Irene** I basically don't care about anything.

**Petrell** I see.

**Irene** I've got no illusions – that's all.

**Petrell** Are you jealous of her men?

**Irene** (*malicious laugh*) What? Freder?

**Petrell** How old are you? You're extremely young. You're extremely pretty. Why've you always got your claws out?

**Irene** (*laughs*) Stop it.

**Petrell** You really are extremely pretty. But you make it hard for people to tell you.

**Irene** I'm serious about my profession, that's all. A woman who studies can't at the same time be a whore. It's disgusting. It's not my conception of learning.

**Petrell** So learning must be immaculately conceived.

**Irene** Don't joke.

**Petrell** And having no one – how immaculate is that?

*Irene is silent.*

You don't have a single person close to you.

**Irene** Learning demands total dedication. The journey has to be made alone.

**Petrell** Clichés.

**Irene** (*smiles*) Dolly.

**Petrell** Call me whatever you like, but it's nothing to do with 'the journey' – it's to do with your inhibitions.

**Irene** That's total nonsense.

**Petrell** And your own feelings of inferiority. You've got this reputation for being proud and unapproachable. But your pride's just repressed fear – you avoid people – you're insecure.

**Irene** (*laughs*) Save it for one of your stories.

**Petrell** If another human being tried to touch you – you'd kill them. Never been with a man, have you?

*Irene is silent.*

I don't believe people are cold by nature. You're just afraid.

**Irene** You can shut up now.

**Petrell** If a beautiful woman lets somebody stroke her hair she's not automatically a prostitute.

**Irene** You should be taking notes. They'll come in useful. For the new rococo writing-table.

**Petrell** (*standing next to her*) Why d'you always have to sneer?

**Irene** Because I find everything so hilarious.

**Petrell** (*cautiously strokes her hair*) You're beautiful, Irene.

**Irene** (*doesn't move*) Don't play games.

**Petrell** (*uncertain of himself*) I'm not playing games.

**Irene** Take away your hand.

**Petrell** I don't want to. (*Embraces her.*)

**Irene** (*doesn't move*) Dolly.

**Petrell** Poor baby – stop punishing yourself.

**Irene** (*softly*) Please let go. What about Marie?

**Petrell** (*smiles*) Marie can't see us.

*Suddenly pulls her close and kisses her.*

**Irene** (*tries to get free*) Please – stop it.

**Petrell** Little liar. Nothing innocent about *you*.

**Irene** (*free*) I won't be taken advantage of.

25

**Petrell** Clichés.

**Irene** You're exploiting the fact we're alone.

**Petrell** Spare me the moral outrage.

**Irene** You hardly know me.

**Petrell** Then give me the opportunity.

**Irene** Don't you need Marie's permission first?

**Petrell** I beg your pardon?

**Irene** She protects her young like a lioness. You'd better take care.

**Petrell** I'm not her son.

**Irene** (*laughs*) Her own little Dolly.

**Petrell** I'm free – I do what I like.

**Irene** (*laughs*) Her precious doll.

**Petrell** Don't provoke me.

**Irene** Go sit at Mummy's rococo writing-table and let's see how quickly inspiration strikes. (*Laughs.*)

**Petrell** Just stop now.

**Irene** (*laughs more and more*) This connection between intellectual work and a piece of furniture – it's completely sick. This is the mentality that's poisoning scientific thought – a sad little slut and an ambitious peasant girl from some Bavarian village [*are prime examples*].

**Petrell** Jealous of Marie as well? I pity you.

**Irene** You're not like them. With the right kind of education you could've become something.

**Petrell** I'm not ambitious.

**Irene** You're lying. Your writing's terrible. But sometimes, for just a few lines, you can suddenly hear an individual voice. It's a shame.

**Petrell** D'you really give my scribbling that much thought?

**Irene** It's a real shame.

**Petrell** I'm not that old.

**Irene** You could have power and glory.

**Petrell** (*ironic*) Power and glory.

**Irene** Laugh if you want – but the truth is, is every intellectual's secretly consumed by ambition.

**Petrell** I'm not secretly consumed.

**Irene** You're not anything at all. You're still cuddled up to Marie. You know nothing about loneliness or tortured nights or work or despair – you just let your sweetheart go on mothering you.

**Petrell** Are you serious or still sneering?

**Irene** I'm serious. (*Looks at him.*)

**Petrell** (*after a pause*) You're serious.

**Irene** (*softly*) Yes.

**Petrell** Irene.

**Irene** Please don't touch me.

**Petrell** You're confusing me.

**Irene** (*laughs*) Keep your hands to yourself. D'you have to start pawing a woman the moment you think she might like you?

**Petrell** Might you like me then?

**Irene** (*suddenly*) There's someone next door.

**Petrell** (*opens Desiree's door*) Herr Freder.

**Irene** (*startled*) Freder?

**Freder** (*from Desiree's room*) Do come in, Petrell.

**Petrell** I'm with Irene. So sorry to disturb you.

*He closes the door.*

**Irene** (*quickly*) He heard us.

**Petrell** He's lying on the couch by the other wall.

**Irene** I warned you about him.

**Petrell** You warn me about everyone.

**Irene** It's right to be cautious.

**Petrell** Thus denying yourself all joy in life.

**Irene** (*laughs*) Joy?

**Petrell** Do I have to translate?

**Irene** A lonely and desperate journey – if it's productive – that's my idea of joy.

**Petrell** Puritan.

**Irene** We really don't understand each other, do we. How long have you known Marie?

**Petrell** Two years.

**Irene** So you were –

**Petrell** – still at university – a student who hated studying. Marie made my life beautiful. I owe her a lot.

**Irene** (*contemptuous*) At least you're grateful.

**Petrell** Without her I'd've starved – literally starved.

**Irene** So she offered you her breast.

**Petrell** (*angry*) That is disgusting.

**Irene** Every reasonable human being seems disgusting to the person who sees through them. You'd be in a totally different position by now if Marie / hadn't – [*protected you*].

**Petrell** I'd've starved to death.

**Irene** Nobody starves to death. Before you do that you wake up and find out who you really are. No one offered me their breast – and I didn't starve.

**Petrell** You've lived like a dog.

**Irene** (*laughs*) Thank God.

**Petrell** I don't envy you.

**Irene** It's why I'm invincible.


SCENE NINE

*Freder enters from Desiree's room.*

**Freder** (*laughs*) Plotting, are we?

  *Irene picks up a book.*

**Petrell** We're waiting for Marie.

**Freder** Of course.

  *Petrell stretches out again.*

Been inspecting the room?

**Petrell** No.

**Freder** Spotless from top to bottom. Our fully-fledged doctor's celebration mad.

**Petrell** She's allowed to be happy.

29

**Freder** Here's to health, happiness, and a long life.

**Petrell** Cheers.

**Freder** That Marie of yours is a very lucky lady.

**Petrell** Science would argue that 'health' doesn't exist.

**Freder** Little Miss Science is reading her nice new book. Let's not disturb her.

**Irene** I'm not arguing anything. (*Goes on reading.*)

**Freder** But wasn't that your voice just now woke me up?

**Irene** I've always thought you listened behind doors.

**Freder** And spy through keyholes.

**Petrell** (*uneasy*) Really?

**Freder** (*watching him*) Of course.

**Irene** (*quickly*) We've nothing to hide.

**Freder** Nothing I didn't already know.

**Irene** (*laughs*) Don't let him intimidate you, Herr Petrell.

**Freder** Don't you mean Dolly?

**Petrell** I beg your pardon?

**Freder** And you are his sweet little Poppet.

**Irene** You're drunk. (*Goes on reading.*)

**Freder** Two little dollies playing with each other, mmm?

**Irene** (*gets up*) Would you please show me out, Herr Petrell.

**Freder** What a handsome young man our Dolly is.

**Petrell** (*gets up*) I thought we were waiting for Marie.

**Irene** We can wait downstairs.

**Freder** (*laughs*) Whatever will she think?

**Irene** That your presence drove us out.

**Freder** Poor Poppet.

**Irene** Come on.

**Petrell** Stop acting the fool, please.

**Freder** I'm waiting for Desiree.

**Irene** Desiree's room's next door.

**Freder** Is that so.

**Irene** This is ridiculous. (*Sits down again.*)

**Freder** (*Pause*) What is it you're reading? (*Stretches out.*)

    *Irene does not reply.*

Come and sit here with me, Petrell. I've taken your seat.

**Petrell** Please don't get up.

**Freder** If she was just a bit less malignant.

**Petrell** You shouldn't provoke her.

**Freder** Such a pretty little thing.

**Irene** You can keep your tasteless remarks to yourself.

**Freder** (*laughs*) Back on form.

**Petrell** D'you think Marie's staying till the end of the exam?

**Freder** Doubt it.

**Irene** I'll tell you what I *will* predict, Petrell: Desiree will get a distinction.

**Freder** Desiree gets distinctions in everything.

**Irene** (*scornful*) You should know.

**Freder** That girl's a real all-rounder.

**Irene** Spare us the details.

**Freder** (*laughs*) Now who's being tasteless.

   *Irene reads.*

What're you going to give Marie?

**Petrell** I haven't decided yet.

**Freder** (*points to the brandy*) From me.

**Irene** Marie doesn't drink on principle.

**Freder** Then Dolly should change her principles.

**Irene** He's too busy adopting them.

**Freder** So we're in agreement, my Poppet.

**Irene** Oh do shut up.

**Petrell** Actually, Marie's got such a healthy constitution –

**Irene** Got *what*?

**Freder** Exactly. There's no such thing as a 'healthy constitution'.

**Irene** There's certainly nothing healthy about being young. Your mind's still half drugged by sleep.

**Petrell** (*softly*) A mind still half drugged by sleep. That's beautiful, Irene.

**Irene** You're just being seduced by words. Being young is a danger zone. Being young means potential proximity / to death.

**Petrell** Being young is the one great adventure of our lives.

**Freder** You're interrupting her to say the same thing.

**Irene** He's all fired up for his rococo writing-table.

**Petrell** Irene.

**Irene** (*quickly*) I'm sorry.

**Petrell** D'you know that marvellous thing from Novalis? 'Nothing so distinguishes man from nature as his addiction to his own sickness and pain.'

**Irene** Novalis was a neurotic.

**Freder** (*smokes*) I'm conducting an interesting experiment. I'm getting someone to the point where I can make them steal for me.

**Petrell** You're a danger to society.

**Freder** All scientific knowledge is a danger to society.

**Irene** You're no scientist.

**Freder** Show me the evidence.

**Irene** (*agitated*) I think you're –

**Freder** (*sits up*) Yes? Say it.

**Irene** I don't think I ought to.

**Freder** Come on, Poppet.

**Irene** I think you have a criminal nature.

**Freder** (*laughs*) Goes with the profession.

**Irene** You don't have a profession.

**Freder** You're getting upset because you're afraid of me.

**Irene** You are seriously deluded.

**Freder** Afraid. You know quite well mine is the only way. To create means to live dangerously. Not just in theory, my Poppet. Acquiring knowledge doesn't mean sticky-fingered leafing through textbooks – as you very well know – that's why you protect yourself.

**Irene** Protect myself from you, yes – you belong in prison.

**Freder** Every truly great individual belongs in prison.

**Irene** That's ridiculous.

**Freder** You cling on to books because an instinct warns you away from the true path. But you know exactly what the true path is. You're not *totally* stupid.

**Irene** (*jumps up*) I'm not listening to any more of this.

**Freder** (*to Petrell*) I've already half seduced her.

**Irene** (*wild*) Just you leave him alone.

**Freder** (*laughs*) Poor Dolly.

**Irene** For you nothing's sacred.

**Freder** Dolly might be corrupted.

**Petrell** Corrupted?

**Irene** Don't listen to him.

**Freder** Don't listen, Dolly.

**Irene** I'm not listening either.

**Freder** Now you're lying.

   *Irene turns away from him.*

Would you like to observe my experiment?

**Irene** We're not participating in your crimes.

**Freder** Tonight at eleven – if the coast's clear.

**Petrell** Why 're you teasing her like this?

**Freder** Just you and me – in the interests of science.

34

**Irene** (*to Petrell*) Don't rise to the bait.

**Petrell** You're being cruel.

**Freder** I'm simply pursuing my studies.

**Petrell** What – now?

**Freder** Surprise you, Dolly?

**Irene** Total rubbish.

**Freder** 'Even in the sciences one cannot simply *know* – one must always first *do*.'

**Irene** Total rubbish.

**Freder** (*laughs*) Goethe, actually.

**Petrell** (*amazed*) Goethe?

**Freder** He didn't just write 'The Erl-King'.* Or is Dolly not allowed to know that either?*

**Irene** (*to Petrell*) Are we really staying here?

**Freder** Drop the play-act, Poppet. You're putting up a magnificent defence. You're the healthiest of us all. Even healthier than the marvellous Marie. The difference is: you understand temptation.

**Petrell** Can we talk about something else please.

**Freder** Come on – she's enjoying it. Whoever lets the limits of the law dictate the limits of knowledge turns into a pillar of the establishment. You – young lady – are well qualified to become a substantial pillar.

**Petrell** Enough now.

**Freder** I've still not qualified as a doctor.

**Petrell** You're certainly taking your time.

* The poem set to music by Schubert.

**Freder** Twelve years.

**Petrell** Romance of the eternal student.

**Freder** You're an idiot – if you don't mind my saying.

**Petrell** (*laughs*) Be my guest.

**Freder** If I was a woman, I'd fall in love with you myself – just like poor Poppet here.

**Petrell** Irene is not in love with me.

**Freder** Wake up, Dolly. This little-boy thing of yours drives women completely insane. As you must surely realise. Wasn't Dizzy in love with you?

*Irene takes note of this.*

**Petrell** Never.

**Freder** I'm not jealous.

**Petrell** Really – never.

**Freder** You could arouse the maternal even in Dizzy.


### SCENE TEN

*Alt.*

*Freder stretches out again.*

**Alt** Party girl not here?

**Petrell** Desiree's got an exam.

**Freder** Petrell, give me a cigarette would you?

**Alt** (*soft*) What the hell's going on?

**Irene** (*caught out*) I'm sorry?

**Alt** You should watch out.

**Irene** (*laughs*) I don't know what you mean.

**Freder** (*to Petrell*) I'm curious. So Desiree / didn't ever – [*drop any hints*].

**Petrell** You want me to swear?

**Freder** Women all come sniffing after you.

**Petrell** Desiree hardly looks at me.

**Freder** She's had too many bad experiences with sensitive young men.

**Alt** I won't allow it.

**Irene** You're completely wrong.

**Alt** She's going to find out.

**Irene** I'm not afraid of some peasant.

**Freder** You claim indifference but that's just an act. It's your feminine weapon. (*Points across the room.*) Poppet's feminine weapon's her arrogance.

**Petrell** Stop calling her Poppet.

**Freder** (*laughs*) You're very easily disillusioned.

**Petrell** What d'you mean?

**Freder** If one little word can sully your ideal.

**Irene** This is none of your business.

**Alt** And you've no business going up to his room.

**Irene** You have a disgusting mind – I pity you.

**Alt** What were you doing so early this morning in his room?

**Irene** (*laughs*) I wanted to see the rococo writing-table.

**Freder**  Marie's feminine weapon's her marvellous good health. Other people use their helplessness to protect them. But basically we're all the same: pitiful bastards.

**Petrell**  I actually need to go home now.

**Freder**  To work.

**Petrell**  How did you guess.

**Freder**  The new writing-table.

**Petrell**  Now you're mocking me.

**Freder**  Great intentions are one thing – perseverance another.

**Petrell**  I want to write a great novel.

**Freder**  And you're feeling inspired.

**Petrell**  You'll be the main protagonist.

*Freder laughs.*

**Irene**  I was up there for less than three minutes – just to collect him.

**Alt**  But now you're wondering [*if it was wise*].

**Irene**  If every innocent little thing / I do – [*is going to attacked*].

**Alt**  This was not innocent.

**Irene**  You really / believe I'd – [*throw myself at someone*].

**Alt**  The intention was not innocent.

**Irene**  I pity you.

**Marie** (*enters*) Alt? How lovely.

*She takes off her hat and jacket.*

**Alt** Congratulations.

**Freder** Hear hear.

**Petrell** (*softly*) It's true, isn't it?

**Irene** What?

**Petrell** What Freder said.

**Irene** Not here.

**Petrell** You are in love with me.

**Irene** Please not here.

**Alt** Where's the lovely Desiree?

**Irene** Getting another distinction I assume.

**Marie** I only took her up to the entrance.

**Freder** Failing something would actually do her good.

**Marie** You're being very quiet, Dolly.

*Goes to Petrell.*

**Irene** You don't wear silk stockings in an operating theatre.

**Freder** Why not?

**Petrell** Oh by the way thanks for the writing-table.

**Marie** When did it come?

**Petrell** This morning. I was still asleep.

**Marie** Beautiful isn't it?

**Petrell** Very beautiful. They had to wake me up.

**Marie** Are you pleased?

**Petrell** Too beautiful almost.

**Marie** You'll soon get used to it.

**Petrell** Yes.

**Marie** Are you alright? Where're you going to put it?

**Petrell** In the bedroom.

**Marie** (*laughs*) I guessed you would. So tell me.

**Petrell** What?

**Marie** Why you're being so unfriendly.

**Petrell** It's not important.

**Marie** Tell me.

**Petrell** (*fierce*) Stop interrogating me.

**Marie** Then you stop being strange.

**Petrell** You're acting just like my mother.

**Marie** (*laughs*) You're funny.

**Petrell** I get enough of this from my *own* mother.

**Marie** That's not nice, Dolly.

**Petrell** 'Letting my sweetheart mother me' – horrible.

**Irene** (*who has been listening*) Are we in the way?

**Petrell** I'm sorry?

**Irene** We can always leave.

**Freder** (*shouts out*) The sea! The sea!

**Irene** What?

**Freder** The sea! The sea!

**Alt** Just humour him.

**Freder** It's the Greek war cry.* Forgotten your classics?

**Irene** Very funny.

**Freder** The battle begins.

**Irene** It's the alcohol.

**Freder** Into position – Dolly in the middle – prepare to fire.

**Marie** Stop being so stupid.

**Freder** Forward march, Poppet. This we must see.

**Marie** (*laughs*) Who on earth's Poppet?

**Freder** Irene, of course.

**Irene** Please shut up.

**Freder** Young Dolly's very own personal Poppet. (*Whistles.*)

**Alt** (*holds Irene back*) Don't – she'll go for you.

**Freder** (*whistles*) Well come on.

   *Marie walks over to Freder.*

Don't come blaming me.

**Marie** How dare you [*say that about Irene and Petrell*].

**Freder** Give your young man a bit of attention.

**Marie** Get out.

**Freder** Or why not just dump him.

---

* *Thálatta! Thálatta!* Exclamation by soldiers on reaching the Black Sea. From Xenophon, *Anabasis*.

*Suddenly puts his arms round Marie.*

He's not right for you.

**Marie** (*tears herself away*) Don't you touch me!

**Freder** That sterile little madam needs a good slap on the arse.

**Irene** I don't have to put up with this. (*Rushes off.*)

**Freder** (*laughs*) Oh I think you do.

**Marie** What [*the hell is going on*]?

**Petrell** We should get her back. (*Rushes off.*)

**Marie** (*stunned*) No. [*I don't believe this is happening.*]

*Freder continues to whistle softly.*

What's going on?

*She goes.*

**Alt** That's quite a horrible scene you've caused.

**Freder** (*looks at him; after a pause*) I think she'll feel more comfortable with you, Herr Alt.

*He goes. Marie hurries back in.*

**Marie** They've already gone down the stairs. (*Takes hat and coat.*)

**Alt** Two steps at a time.

**Marie** (*laughs*) Can you please explain what's happening?

**Alt** Where is it you're going?

**Marie** I'll catch them up.

**Alt** (*sharply*) No. Come and sit down.

*Marie looks at him, amazed.*

Marie – come here.

**Marie** I don't understand.

**Alt** Let them run off.

**Marie** They won't be running. Not in the street.

**Alt** Maybe they are running – even in the street.

*Marie's body goes limp.*

Sit here with me.

*Marie doesn't move.*

Put down the hat.

*Marie does so mechanically.*

And the jacket.

*Marie sits. Pause.*

**Marie** You're imagining things [*about Petrell and Irene*].

**Alt** Make yourself comfortable. We've got time.

**Marie** (*laughs*) No, sweetheart – she's far too unimportant [*for this to be true*].

**Alt** It's not the important things that ruin us.

**Marie** It can't be true.

**Alt** I lost my job at the general hospital, did time in prison. A terminally ill child was suffering so much, I ended its life. Gave it morphine instead of camphor. Are you listening?

**Marie** Morphine instead of camphor.

**Alt** It destroyed my life. And I'd do it again. D'you understand?

**Marie** You'd do it again.

**Alt** I'd do it again.

**Marie** You'd do it again. (*Laughs.*) No, you're not being serious.

**Alt** And you're being far too serious about that nice young man of yours.

**Marie** So I just – what – tear him out of my heart?

**Alt** Convicted of manslaughter – two years in prison. You'd've done the same.

**Marie** Me?

**Alt** It makes it very clear how out of date the laws are.

**Marie** I'm going insane.

**Alt** We're living on obsolete ideas. It's outrageous. Are you listening?

**Marie** It's outrageous.

**Alt** It's outrageous.

**Marie** It's outrageous. (*Laughs.*) He's probably sitting with her right now.

**Alt** Fists clenched.

**Marie** (*mechanically*) Fists clenched.

**Alt** Become aware.

**Marie** Become aware.

**Alt** Wake up. Clinging to others is weak.

**Marie** Living like Freder is strong.

**Alt** Fully conscious of your own self.

**Marie** Fully conscious. (*Laughs.*) Rhythmic gymnastics. We're both of us insane.

**Alt** Now you're coming to your senses

**Marie** Now I'm coming to my senses.

**Alt** Erasing him totally from your mind.

**Marie** You're turning into an animal like Freder.

**Alt** Freder's no animal.

**Marie** A criminal.

**Alt** Aren't I one too?

**Marie** (*amazed*) Are you? She's with him.

**Alt** With him.

**Marie** With him?

*She starts to laugh – her laughter quickly grows more intense.*

And there's me scrubbing the floor – not even an hour ago – for who? Laugh – come on. The spotless room.

*She takes the bottle next to her and throws it into the mirror.*

See that shatter. Did you hear that crack? To hell with the spotless room – it's a pigsty. Let's live like pigs. Laugh – come on.

**Alt** (*wild*) I'm laughing, I'm laughing.

**Marie** Let's live like pigs.

**Alt** Let's live like pigs.

**Marie** Before I was just dreaming. Idiot. Idiot. Like pigs. Laugh – come on. Pigsty idiot. Pigsty idiot. Come on! I WANT TO HEAR YOU LAUGH!

*She collapses. Alt catches her and strokes her hair.*

*Curtain.*

# Act Two

## SCENE ONE

*Evening. Flowers in the room.*

*Marie and Desiree are dancing to the gramophone.*

**Desiree** Come on – smaller steps.

**Marie** (*laughs*) I can't. You're so impatient.

**Desiree** You can do it – you can do anything.

**Marie** You terrible flatterer.

**Desiree** Marion.

*Marie laughs.*

My little Marion.

**Marie** (*laughs*) Can't do it.

**Desiree** Relax your back. Your hips have to be nice and loose.

**Marie** Easier said . . . [*than done*].

**Desiree** Cold shower, quick rub with a towel, and Swedish gymnastics every morning.

**Marie** As if I had time / for that.

**Desiree** Make time. Doing exercise blocks out all that pointless thinking. (*Laughs.*) That was my foot.

**Marie** Again.

**Desiree** I forgive you everything.

**Marie** D'you still love me?

**Desiree** Silly girl.

**Marie** (*stops dancing*) What was it?

**Desiree** What was what?

**Marie** (*laughs*) '. . . an inner and overpowering desire to finally break the chains of habit.'

**Desiree** How can you know that pathetic letter off by heart?

**Marie** '. . . to run wild as the prairie mustang from the locked cage.'

**Desiree** The cage was you.

**Marie** 'Since we all yearn a little for the prairie . . .'

**Desiree** Do stop.

**Marie** The cage was me.

**Desiree** And the prairie has red hair.

**Marie** Look – look – his exact words . . .

   *She finds the place.*

**Desiree** For godsake.

   *She winds up the gramophone again.*

**Marie** (*reads the letter*) 'It was an inner and overpowering desire to finally break the chains of habit . . .'

**Desiree** Listen.

**Marie** Chains of habit.

**Desiree** This one's from Java. [*The dance.*]

**Marie** Perhaps he's right.

**Desiree** Just let him go. Listen – isn't that lovely?

**Marie**  I am letting him go.

**Desiree**  Come on.

*They dance again.*

**Marie**  Perhaps he's right.

**Desiree**  Bigger steps here.

**Marie**  Like this?

**Desiree**  Fantastic.

**Marie**  Twenty-four hours ago I wouldn't've believed it. How can we forget so fast?

**Desiree**  You've no idea how fast.

**Marie**  Or do we just think we do?

**Desiree**  (*brutal*) If you won't concentrate, you can't dance.

*Turns gramophone off.*

**Marie**  (*quickly*) I am concentrating.

**Desiree**  You're being self-indulgent [*in memories*].

**Marie**  I'm just thinking about what Alt said to me yesterday.

**Desiree**  If Alt was actually a man – he'd be a total god.

**Marie**  He *is* a man.

**Desiree**  (*laughs*) You're still so naive. I could take a bath in front of him, like he was some old woman. Alt doesn't do sex. (*Stretches out.*)

**Marie**  So what about his child?

**Desiree**  He just had a child for the sake of having one. Which is even stranger for a man than it is for a woman: male but motherly.

**Marie** He was hard on me yesterday.

**Desiree** Male but motherly – soft, but can be very strict.

**Marie** He sticks his finger down your throat till it all comes out.

**Desiree** If ever I just can't go on –

**Marie** (*by Desiree*) What?

**Desiree** I'll go to him.

**Marie** Can't go on?

**Desiree** (*kisses her hand*) Marion.

**Marie** (*pulls her hand away*) No.

**Desiree** Turn out the light. Let's dream.

*Marie is silent.*

Come on – let's go to bed.

**Marie** No – I don't feel tired. (*Pause.*) Tomorrow's my party.

**Desiree** That's so beautifully childish.

**Marie** When you really really want something to be good, you always end up looking like a stupid child. Freder was the great destroyer of my illusions.

**Desiree** You should thank him.

**Marie** I don't want to speak to him.

**Desiree** It would do you good.

**Marie** No.

*Pause.*

**Desiree** You should see Freder when he's lost control.

**Marie** What d'you mean: / 'lost control'?

**Desiree** I'd never've put up with him otherwise. He sucks at your skin like he wants to taste blood. It's not just sex – it's mad – it's animal – it hurts. But those are the only moments in our lives when our poor pathetic bodies get to feel what it might be actually like to die.

**Marie** (*softly*) This is not you, Desiree.

**Desiree** One tiny step beyond sex, one tiny step beyond pain – and you'd never wake up.

*Kisses her passionately.*

How wonderful that would be.

**Marie** (*sobbing, pulls Desiree towards her*) You're not to die, you're not to die.

**Desiree** Let's die together, Marion.

*They are sitting pressed close together.*

Sometimes you pretend everything's fine, but then you wake up and it's all exactly the same. Always always exactly the same. Why bother? (*Pause.*) If just one of those times I'd whispered to Freder: bite my neck – kill me – he'd've done it – yes – much safer to be killed. But I was too afraid. Because I got Freder trained – I just had to make up my mind – but I was too afraid. Two little words just as he's losing control. Two little words – kill me – and he'd do it – bite me – bite into my neck. He knows that's the critical moment.

**Marie** Please don't.

**Desiree** I've got him trained like an animal: all he needs is his cue.

**Marie** (*gently frees herself from Desiree*) No, sweetheart.

**Desiree** And one day he'll do it. Only not with me, unfortunately. We missed our moment.

**Marie** You're not to die.

**Desiree** (*smiles*) Your eyes are completely blue.

**Marie** Please don't.

**Desiree** You're so beautiful, Marion.

**Marie** (*smiles*) Let's just both quietly sit.

**Desiree** Just you and me.

**Marie** Just you and me. No talking.

   *Pause.*

**Desiree** (*smiles*) You know something . . .

**Marie** What?

**Desiree** Maybe I should be . . .

**Marie** Should be what?

**Desiree** (*laughs*) Should be taking a look at the hideous volume.

**Marie** Anatomy?

**Desiree** The exam's in three weeks.

**Marie** But yesterday it went / brilliantly.

**Desiree** It's ridiculous – other people cram day and night and still fail. I don't understand.

**Marie** I used to spend days and nights cramming.

**Desiree** Wasn't it horrid?

**Marie** No, it was lovely.

**Desiree** (*takes a chocolate out of the box*) Eat.

    *Both eat.*

Shall we dance or go to bed?

**Marie** It's too early. It's so nice sitting here. Lucy can make us some tea. (*Rings bell.*)

**Desiree** I'll go to bed and you come and sit.

**Marie** Are you tired?

**Desiree** You don't just go to bed when you're tired – you go when you're feeling good. I love bed. I feel safe in bed – like coming home.

**Marie** Go on then, sweetheart.

**Desiree** Don't keep me waiting too long.

    *Goes into her room.*

**Marie** (*sneaks look at letter*) '. . . wild as the prairie mustang from the locked cage . . .'


### SCENE TWO

*Lucy enters.*

**Marie** Make us some tea, would you? What is it?

**Lucy** (*smiles*) Frau Schimmelbrot.

**Marie** Oh?

**Lucy** Frau Schimmelbrot's gone out.

**Marie** Is there no tea then?

**Lucy** Oh yes [*there is*].

**Marie** (*offers her a chocolate*) Chocolate?

**Lucy** Thank you. We're both from Passau.

**Marie** Oh really?

**Lucy** It's on your registration form.

**Marie** Why've you been looking at my registration form?

**Lucy** Ages ago.

**Marie** (*watches her*) Well, how lovely you're from Passau too.

**Lucy** I didn't dare say. My father's worked for yours. My father's a carpenter.

**Marie** Why 're you so cheerful today?

**Lucy** So your father's a master-craftsman.

**Marie** Builds houses – yes.

**Lucy** Thought so.

**Marie** Why 're you so cheerful today?

**Lucy** It's such a lovely evening.

**Marie** Are you going out?

**Lucy** (*smiles*) Maybe.

**Marie** Then I'll make the tea.

**Lucy** I can't go yet. My fiancé's worked for your father too.

**Marie** You've got a fiancé?

**Lucy** My fiancé's a decorator.

**Marie** Why did you leave Passau?

**Lucy** I'm one of six children.

**Marie** Are you getting married soon?

**Lucy** Not till I go back. That's lovely you're from Passau too.

**Marie** (*laughs*) Why's it lovely?

**Lucy** (*points at Desiree's door*) I wouldn't like to be from the same town as the young lady.

**Marie** Oh really?

**Lucy** But Passau's lovely. – All my brothers and sisters are from Passau. – Now they've all left.

*She goes. Marie winds up the gramophone and sits next to it.*


SCENE THREE

*Irene.*

**Irene** Can I talk to you?

*Marie is silent.*

Won't take a moment.

*Marie is silent.*

We can stand if you prefer.

**Marie** (*quickly*) Sorry.

*They sit.*

**Irene** Could you maybe turn off the gramophone?

**Marie** Is it bothering you?

**Irene** [*It's*] Your choice. I don't want any misunder-standings.

**Marie** You like clarity.

**Irene** Has Herr Petrell not come to see you yet?

**Marie** Rubbish –

**Irene** If you're not even going to let me / *speak.*

**Marie** – Petrell would never come and see me. He's a coward.

**Irene** That depends who's influencing him.

**Marie** (*laughs*) Really?

**Irene** No man is an island.

**Marie** And under your influence he'll be courageous.

**Irene** You're upset.

**Marie** You'll teach him to be a hero.

**Irene** D'you really enjoy this music?

*Marie is silent.*

I can hardly hear myself talk.

**Marie** Weird how someone can change in just twenty-four hours.

**Irene** What d'you mean?

**Marie** Your face has got rounder. Softer and rounder. You're beautiful.

*She gets up and turns off the gramophone.*

**Irene** Thank God for that.

**Marie** Make yourself at home.

**Irene** We need to deal with this objectively.

**Marie** Of course: objectively.

**Irene** Herr Petrell –

**Marie**  Objectively.

**Irene**  Herr Petrell –

**Marie**  Herr Petrell? – You mean your new boyfriend.

**Irene**  You're wrong. It's not like that.

**Marie**  I got a letter from him this morning.

**Irene**  I know.

**Marie**  (*looks at her*) Does he show you his letters? Maybe the two of you composed it together.

**Irene**  He has his own style.

**Marie**  Absolutely. 'Prairie mustang in the cage.'

**Irene**  He's a poet.

**Marie**  He's a poet.

**Irene**  I wanted to offer you our friendship.

**Marie**  Thank you.

**Irene**  You've done a great deal for him.

**Marie**  Thank you.

**Irene**  You've helped him through very difficult times.

**Marie**  (*agitated*) Thank you.

**Irene**  He'll never forget that. He speaks about you very very warmly. You were more to him than just a mother.

**Marie**  (*beside herself*) Will you shut up now.

**Irene**  I don't understand you.

**Marie**  You don't understand me.

**Irene**  He can't just cut you out of his life. You mean far too much to him.

**Marie** To the 'prairie mustang'.

**Irene** That's just a literary turn of phrase.

**Marie** Whose turn of phrase? Yours by any chance?

**Irene** You're impossible to talk to.

**Marie** I'm not a reptile.

**Irene** No one's saying you are. (*She gets up.*)

**Marie** Don't get up.

**Irene** Marie.

**Marie** I'm not a reptile.

**Irene** What d'you mean: reptile?

**Marie** Tell me – come on – what is it you want?

**Irene** I wanted to offer you our friendship.

**Marie** Thank you.

**Irene** Which I have now done.

**Marie** Thank you.

**Irene** And until you can be more reasonable –

**Marie** Sit down.

**Irene** – I'll leave you to your musical evening.

**Marie** Sit down.

**Irene** I've got things to do.

**Marie** Sit down.

**Irene** Don't play the teacher with me.

**Marie** Sit down.

**Irene** You seem / to be – [*upset*].

**Marie** (*beside herself*) SIT DOWN.

**Irene** (*sits*) I don't understand.

**Marie** (*tears off Irene's hat*) We're having tea together.

**Irene** I've got things to do.

**Marie** But now you're with me.

**Irene** (*uncertain*) I won't be intimidated.

**Marie** How kind of you to visit.

**Irene** I won't be made fun of.

**Marie** (*offers her a chocolate*) Chocolate?

**Irene** I don't eat sweets.

**Marie** From Desiree. She gave me this box today. Nice, don't you think? The flowers are from Desiree too. Look at them.

**Irene** She's a very nice person.

**Marie** No – it's a very nice box.

**Irene** I'm not sure I follow.

**Marie** So – 'your friendship'.

**Irene** Give it some thought.

**Marie** Meaning what – 'your friendship'.

**Irene** Give it some thought. When you feel more calm.

**Marie** I'm perfectly calm. Was this his idea?

**Irene** That's not relevant.

**Marie** There's nothing in the letter [*about friendship*].

**Irene** We only thought of it later.

**Marie** We?

**Irene** It was obvious – it didn't need to be spelt out.

**Marie** I don't find it obvious.

**Irene** Not when you've been with him for two years?

**Marie** So you had to point that out to him as well?

**Irene** It's like you think he's an idiot.

**Marie** He's thoughtless about others, but he's not a bad person.

**Irene** No one's saying he is.

**Marie** All the same it would never 've occurred to him to come here offering me his 'friendship'. That's *your* idea.

**Irene** That's not relevant.

**Marie** It's extremely relevant. Because you *are* a bad person.

**Irene** Say what you like.

**Marie** You have a thirst for control.

*Irene laughs.*

You calculate levels of emotion.

**Irene** I don't think so.

**Marie** You've taught him the level of gratitude towards *me*, which is not dangerous for *you*.

**Irene** Go on – this obviously does you good.

**Marie** You have goals, but no emotions. You're a reptile.

**Irene** So I'm a reptile [*i.e. so what*].

**Marie** You know your objective.

**Irene** I'm not denying it.

59

**Marie**  Your ambition's like a machine – you've got your objective and no scruples about how you reach it.

**Irene**  I've worked hard for it.

**Marie**  I know.

**Irene**  I didn't get my education in bed –

**Marie**  I know.

**Irene**  – but in an unheated room.

**Marie**  You've gone hungry to reach your objective.

**Irene**  I have gone hungry.

**Marie**  Because it made you proud.

**Irene**  Going hungry?

**Marie**  Going hungry.

**Irene**  Made me *proud*? Ridiculous.

**Marie**  You tell everyone you went hungry so you could study.

**Irene**  Because a young woman who's not ugly can find other ways of making ends meet.

**Marie**  No one's ever accused you of that.

**Irene**  Young people get accused of absolutely everything. That's why it's no use us just surviving – we have to win. That's the secret – that's what finding our own path means.

**Marie**  Is this what you came to say to me?

**Irene**  We could still be friends.

**Marie**  Are you saying you need me?

*Irene looks at her, uncertain.*

Both stand by me, would you?

**Irene** If you want.

**Marie** I don't want.

**Irene** Then forgive the intrusion. (*Gets up.*)

**Marie** I never want to see either of you ever again.

**Irene** We'll respect that.

**Marie** I hate this whole act of yours.

**Irene** Please [*don't*].

**Marie** This kindness, this readiness to help – it's all an act. You just want to show off your power. I'm not impressed.

**Irene** Let's part on good terms, shall we?

**Marie** Common as muck – Sally from the alley.

**Irene** There's no need to be abusive.

**Marie** Well, isn't that your name?

**Irene** So what if my name's Sally?

**Marie** Then why call yourself Irene? Everything about you 's an act.

*Irene tries to get to the door.*

Who ever heard of a porter's daughter called Irene.

**Irene** Let me out.

**Marie** (*blocking her way*) Sit.

**Irene** You're out of your mind.

**Marie** Sit.

**Irene** Let me out. (*Touches her.*)

**Marie** (*pushes her away*) I said sit.

**Irene** I'll scream for help.

**Marie** Scream away, Sally – he won't hear you downstairs.

**Irene** (*approaches her*) I won't have people blocking my way.

**Marie** (*savagely grabs Irene's hair*) Here's the prairie – yes? The red, red prairie. Why d'you have to grow your hair?

**Irene** GET OFF OF ME.

**Marie** (*laughs*) Just to be different. It's all an act.

**Irene** I'll smash your face.

*They fight.*

**Marie** (*laughing*) Waiting downstairs – the kind of man you can train to do anything. Well spotted, Sally. Sally from the stinking alley.

*She drags Irene across the room and ties her by her hair to the leg of a cupboard.*

The sea! The sea! Let's play prairie Indians! (*Laughs more and more.*) Lash her to the cupboard! Lash the paleface squaw to the prairie cupboard! PALE – FACE – RED – HEAD – RED – HEAD – RED HEAD – YOU'RE – DEAD. (*Jumps up.*) Now let's go fetch the wild mustang. (*Goes out.*)

**Irene** (*screams after Marie, beside herself*) YOU'RE THE ONE 'LL END UP KILLING YOURSELF.

*She tries to untie her hair.*

## SCENE FOUR

*Freder at Desiree's door.*

**Freder** Why 're you sitting on the floor?

**Irene** She's going to pay for this.

**Freder** You seem to be tied up by the hair.

**Irene** She's going to pay for this.

**Freder** It's not so easy to undo.

**Irene** You're hurting me.

**Freder** You've got thick hair.

**Irene** Leave it – I can do it myself.

**Freder** Thick, beautiful hair.
What were you doing here?

**Irene** We felt sorry for her.

**Freder** If you keep pulling like that it'll just get more tangled. (*Helps again.*)

**Irene** She'll kill him if she finds him.

**Freder** Is he waiting for you downstairs?

**Irene** No, he is not waiting for me downstairs.

**Freder** Somewhere nearby then?

**Irene** Get your hands off me.

**Freder** (*laughs*) In my own good time. The fact is Poppet is you're suddenly at my mercy. I could do anything I want with you – little temptress. Are you ticklish?

**Irene** (*frantic*) GET OFF ME.

**Freder**  Never slept with a man, have you?

**Irene**  You're not my confessor, thank you very much.

**Freder**  First priest – then bed.
   You're tearing great lumps out.

**Irene**  (*free, quickly tidies herself in the mirror*) You'll never see me again. (*She goes.*)

**Freder**  He'll wonder who's been making you so hot and bothered.

   *Goes into Desiree's room.*


### SCENE FIVE

*Lucy enters with a tea tray.*

**Lucy**  (*at Desiree's door*) Shall I bring in the tea?

**Freder**  (*appears*) Who for?

**Lucy**  (*softly*) The young lady – Marie – ordered it.

**Freder**  Put the tray on the table.

   *Lucy puts the tray on the table.*

Is that your Sunday dress?

**Lucy**  Yes.

**Freder**  Come nearer.
Look at me.

**Lucy**  Herr Freder.

**Freder**  Why 're you smiling? Happy?

**Lucy**  Frau Schimmelbrot isn't here.

**Freder**  Where is Frau Schimmelbrot?

**Lucy** I don't know.

**Freder** Has Frau Schimmelbrot gone to a ball?

**Lucy** I don't know.

**Freder** Does she often go out?

**Lucy** No. Hardly.

**Freder** Then she's probably gone to a ball. But what about the rings?

**Lucy** She still hasn't noticed.

**Freder** Then she hasn't gone to a ball, she's visiting poor relations. Why 're you laughing? You don't show your jewellery to poor relations.

**Lucy** (*laughs*) No.

**Freder** You want to go out now?

**Lucy** It's up to you.

**Freder** We've still got time. (*Pours tea.*) Take a seat.

*Lucy laughs.*

**Freder** Why 're you laughing?

**Lucy** I'm so happy.

**Freder** Drink your tea.

*Offers her the chocolates.*

**Lucy** The young lady already gave me one.

**Freder** Drink and eat.

*Suddenly goes into Desiree's room – the door stays open.*

(*Off.*) May I?

*Desiree, off, laughs.*

(*Off.*) It's for our young friend Lucy.

**Desiree** (*off*) You must be joking (*Laughs.*)

**Freder** (*off*) Don't get up. I can manage.

*Lucy strains to listen.*

**Desiree** (*off*) Are you taking her out?

**Freder** Yes.

*Comes back in with powder brush and make-up kit.*

Stay where you are.

**Lucy** (*alarmed*) Herr Freder.

**Freder** Tomorrow I'll buy you your own.

*Sits facing her.*

You have to keep your head up.

**Lucy** (*softly*) I don't know how to do it.

**Freder** I'll show you. Eyes are the most important.

*Begins to make up her face.*

**Lucy** Herr Freder.

**Freder** Why 're you so nervous?

**Lucy** You think it'll suit me?

**Freder** You have to completely trust me.

**Lucy** Yes.

**Freder** Keep your head still. Have you really never used powder before?

**Lucy** No.

**Freder** Natural beauty's a blank canvas.

**Lucy** (*naively*) Yes.

**Freder** Nature's there to be made conform to our wishes. Make-up brings a woman to life.

**Lucy** Yes.

**Freder** You have an exquisite face. But it needs more definition to be really attractive. Nearly finished. Why 're you shaking? Does that tingle?

**Lucy** Herr Freder.

**Freder** (*laughs*) Makes you feel strange, mmm? Makes you want to grab on to me, does it?

*Lucy is silent.*

Now the cheeks.

**Lucy** Now I realise.

**Freder** Realise what?

**Lucy** You think I'm ugly.

**Freder** Rubbish.

**Lucy** Or you wouldn't do this make-up.

**Freder** You're beautiful – it just needs bringing out.

**Lucy** (*still uncertain*) Yes.

**Freder** Natural beauty stinks of soap. Keep your lips still.

**Lucy** (*suddenly*) Herr Freder.

**Freder** What?

**Lucy** You won't want to kiss me any more.

**Freder** (*laughs*) You're mad.

**Lucy** When they're all that disgusting red.

**Freder** Keep still.

**Lucy** Please don't, Herr Freder.

**Freder** (*forces on make-up*) Stupid baby.

**Lucy** Please – not my lips.

**Freder** You're mad if you think I won't want to kiss you.

**Lucy** (*not resisting*) Herr Freder.

**Freder** Now look in the mirror.

**Lucy** (*stands a long time in front of the mirror*) That's not me.

**Freder** It's you at your full potential. See how beautiful you are?

*Lucy is silent.*

Now I'll get you a beautiful coat.

**Lucy** No, Herr Freder, please don't.

**Freder** And a nice little hat.

**Lucy** (*gets dizzy*) No.

**Freder** Then we'll go out together.

*He goes into Desiree's room. Lucy drops into a chair. He returns with Desiree's coat and hat.*

Why 're you crying? Chin up. You'll smudge your eyes. Here – use my handkerchief.

*Lucy dries her eyes. He helps her into the coat.*

You can laugh now, mmm?

*Lucy looks at him.*

Laugh.

*Lucy smiles.*

Laugh properly!

*He kisses her on the mouth.*

**Lucy** (*comforted*) Herr Freder.

**Freder** My little honey-mouth. Happy?

**Lucy** (*laughs warmly*) I'm happy if you are.

**Freder** Now you're beautiful.

**Lucy** And the hat. (*Puts it on.*)

**Freder** Excellent.

*Lucy looks at him.*

Men will fall at your feet.

**Lucy** I feel embarrassed.

**Freder** People will be turning round to stare.

**Lucy** I feel so strange.

**Freder** They'll come up to you and talk.

**Lucy** Not if you're there they won't.

**Freder** But what if I'm not?

**Lucy** You mean you'd just leave me?

**Freder** Wouldn't that be fun?

**Lucy** I'd rather drown myself.

**Freder** And if I don't want you to drown yourself?

**Lucy** Then I won't drown myself.

**Freder** Because you love me.

**Lucy** Because I love you very much.

**Freder** And if I said to you, *let* them talk to you.

**Lucy** (*confused*) I don't understand what you mean.

**Freder** Some nice young man you found appealing.

**Lucy** No, Herr Freder.

**Freder** Look in the mirror. A rich young gentleman could find you very appealing too.

**Lucy** I don't care.

**Freder** You love only me, mmm?
Come on.

**Lucy** Are we going to a fancy-dress ball? I've never been to a fancy-dress ball.

**Freder** Well you're certainly fancily dressed.

**Lucy** (*laughs*) Especially my face.

**Desiree** (*appears at the door*) Let's have a look at you, Lucy.

**Lucy** (*terrified*) Oh my God. (*She goes.*)

**Desiree** She looks *appalling.*

**Freder** (*laughs*) She feels embarrassed.

**Desiree** Are you putting her on the game?

**Freder** Your help has been invaluable. (*He goes.*)


### SCENE SIX

*Marie and Petrell.*

**Marie** Come on. (*To Desiree.*) Leave us alone, please.

*Desiree goes back into her own room. Marie forces Petrell into the room.*

She's not here. And she was waiting for you so sweetly. You weren't fast enough. (*Laughs.*)

**Petrell** Where is Irene?

**Marie** You weren't fast enough. Why were you lurking like that?
Sit down.

**Petrell** (*stays standing*) What is it you want?

**Marie** Certainly not you. Don't you worry.

**Petrell** What is it you want?

**Marie** Sit.

**Petrell** When you've calmed down.

**Marie** I'm perfectly calm.

**Petrell** I know what you're like.

**Marie** Thank you.

**Petrell** Is this really how you want it to end?

**Marie** Save the concerned voice for her.

**Petrell** I want to explain to you.

**Marie** I'd just have to do that – (*clicks fingers*) and you'd never go back to her. You're putty in my hands.

**Petrell** You're impossible to talk to.

**Marie** Why am I impossible to talk to?

**Petrell** What you do 's not talking.

**Marie** Oh? What is it then?

**Petrell** Spitting.

**Marie** (*laughs*) Spitting?

**Petrell** Metaphorically – yes.

**Marie** So she talks –

**Petrell** Oh please.

**Marie** – and I just spit.

**Petrell** I did not say that you spit.

**Marie** You did say that I spit.

**Petrell** What I meant was you're / overexcited.

**Marie** You did say that I spit.

**Petrell** Too excited to talk / calmly.

**Marie** You did say that I spit.

**Petrell** Believe what you want.

**Marie** Don't you tell me what to believe.

**Petrell** Why did you drag me here?

**Marie** So you could collect Irene.

**Petrell** You're lying.

**Marie** So you could take her away.

**Petrell** She'd already gone: you must've followed her.

**Marie** (*laughs*) She had not 'already gone'.

**Petrell** She would've stopped you attacking me like this.

**Marie** (*laughs*) I can be hard to stop.

**Petrell** You ran after her: you must've caught her up.

**Marie** You'd make a hopeless detective. Look – perhaps there's some bit of her left in the room.

**Petrell** Better we talk some other time.

**Marie** Some bit of Prairie in the room.

**Petrell** When you've calmed down.

**Marie** Seek, Mustang, seek.

**Petrell** I've had enough. (*Makes to go.*)

**Marie** Seek, Mustang. Prairie – red red Prairie. Cold. Cold. (*Laughs.*) If you go over the the cupboard you'll be getting HOT HOT.

*Pushes him towards the cupboard.*

Use your eyes. See anything? (*Triumphant.*) Ah-ha! The red red Prairie!

*Shows him some of Irene's hair.*

**Petrell** (*shocked*) What on earth were you doing?

**Marie** Playing Indians.

**Petrell** (*horrified*) Marie.

**Marie** (*big laugh*) Playing Indians. On the wide open Prairie – whoa there, Mustang! I scalped her – scalped the red-haired chief.

**Petrell** (*grabs her, horrified*) Marie.

*Marie suddenly quiet, looks at him.*

(*Softly.*) What've you done to her?

*Marie stares at him open-eyed.*

Have you / hurt her?

**Marie** (*softly*) Let go of me.

**Petrell** Have you gone mad?

**Marie** Don't ever touch me again.

**Petrell** I want to know what you've done to her.

**Marie**  Nothing.

**Petrell**  (*tough*) Where's Irene?

**Marie**  (*suddenly*) What if I've murdered her.

**Petrell**  I don't believe you.

**Marie**  I've murdered her.

**Petrell**  I don't believe you.

**Marie**  Just now you were terrified.

**Petrell**  But I don't believe you.

**Marie**  But you *were* terrified.

**Petrell**  I don't think you're capable.

**Marie**  You could be wrong.

**Petrell**  I can see it in your eyes.

**Marie**  Great expert on human nature.

**Petrell**  Where is she?

**Marie**  Lying in the kitchen. The police are on their way. The doctor's in the kitchen too.

**Petrell**  You're hiding her somewhere.

**Marie**  Ask the doctor. I strangled her. If you stay you may be arrested too.

**Petrell**  You've locked her in. Is she in Desiree's room?

**Marie**  I wouldn't ask so many questions if I were you. I'd go to the kitchen. Or are you afraid?

**Petrell**  You enjoy seeing me suffer.

**Marie**  (*changes tack*) She's fine.

**Petrell**  Then where is she?

**Marie**  At home.

**Petrell**  At home?

**Marie**  Or at your place. D'you love her that much?

**Petrell**  So she didn't leave with you?

**Marie**  (*exhausted*) I tied her up so she wouldn't stop me finding you. She'll be very useful. You'll go far. She's very clever.

**Petrell**  (*incredulous*) By the hair?

**Marie**  (*nods*) Tell me when you first fell in love with her.

**Petrell**  It's so *crude*.

**Marie**  Forgive me. D'you love her that much?

**Petrell**  Leave me alone now.

**Marie**  Does it really hurt? Won't you forgive me?

**Petrell**  I'm going now.

**Marie**  Won't you forgive me? Kiss me.

**Petrell**  I have to go now.

**Marie**  Don't – don't hate me for ever. With her help you'll go all the way to the top.

**Petrell**  I always said it was a mistake [*to be together so long*].

**Marie**  Said what was a mistake?

**Petrell**  Goodbye, Marie.

**Marie**  You both coming here – *that* was the mistake. You know me better than she does – you shouldn't've let her talk you into it. Should you? Say something.

**Petrell**  How could you 've done something so *crude*?

**Marie** She'll go all the way to the top as well. You'll both go all the way to the top.

*Petrell makes to go.*

**Marie** (*suddenly*) Hit me then.

**Petrell** You're being mad.

**Marie** Hit me – if you won't forgive me.

**Petrell** You want the whole house to hear?

**Marie** You despise me – say it.

**Petrell** Words are no use to us now.

**Marie** Then hit me.

**Petrell** Don't shout.

**Marie** What do I have to do to make you hit me? I hit that bitch. I tied her up by the hair. I tied her up like a dog. (*Beside herself.*) Hit me.

*Petrell makes for the door.*

Stay where you are. A man who's loved someone for two whole years doesn't just go slinking off. Or was that just an act?

**Petrell** I'm sick of this. (*Opens door.*)

**Marie** (*beside herself*) What about the money?

**Petrell** What money?

**Marie** My money – the money I used to keep you.

**Petrell** (*quickly shuts the door*) The whole house is going to hear.

**Marie** Yes, the whole house is going to hear how for two whole years you lived off of me.

**Petrell** (*pale*) Are you insane?

**Marie** Doesn't like hearing *that*, does he. Who let me buy everything for him? Who let me give lessons late into the night to pay for his meals? Whose suits did I buy – whose books, shoes, shirts, socks?

**Petrell** You'll get your money back.

**Marie** Like hell I will. You won't be getting any handouts from *her*.

**Petrell** I earn money.

**Marie** And who was it trailed round the streets finding you work?

**Petrell** I'm not saying / you didn't.

**Marie** Or got you into that sanatorium for a lung disease that was total fiction.

**Petrell** This is grossly unfair.

**Marie** Unfair how?

**Petrell** You're treating me like a thief.

**Marie** Aren't you a thief?

**Petrell** Marie.

**Marie** Well are you a thief or not?

**Petrell** You don't know what you're saying / any more.

**Marie** You are a thief.

**Petrell** I've had enough. (*Heads for door.*)

**Marie** Then hit me – if you're not a thief.

**Petrell** Want the whole house to come / running, do you.

**Marie**  Hit me.

*Holds him.*

Hit me – if you're not a thief. Don't you care about / me at all?

**Petrell**  You need to stick your head in some cold water.

**Marie**  (*falls to her knees, crying*) Hit me – if you're not a thief.

**Petrell**  I refuse to be part of this.

*Tears himself away.*

**Marie**  I won't let you go till you hit me. I won't let you.

**Petrell**  You belong in the madhouse. (*He goes.*)

**Marie**  Hit me – hit me – hit me.


### SCENE SEVEN

*Desiree enters from her room.*

**Desiree**  (*kneels by her*) Marion.

**Marie**  (*smiles*) Hit me. You're not a thief.

**Desiree**  (*helps her up*) Poor poor baby.

**Marie**  He wouldn't hit me.

**Desiree**  Come on. I'll kiss away those tears.

**Marie**  Yes. Kiss me.

**Desiree**  My little Marion.

**Marie**  He wouldn't hit me. Kiss me harder.

**Desiree**  (*kisses her passionately*) Come on – come to bed – just you and me – all snug and warm.

**Marie** Just you and me.

**Desiree** All snug and warm, like being little. I'll tell you all my secrets, Marion – like two little sisters before they go to sleep.

**Marie** Like two little sisters in the dark before they go to sleep. You're my sister.

**Desiree** And you're mine.

*They hold each other.*

*Curtain.*

# Act Three

## SCENE ONE

*Evening.*

*Marie, Desiree, Freder, Alt.*

**Freder** (*stretched out*) My liver doesn't feel right.

**Alt** Drink less.

**Freder** My liver's affecting my brain.

**Desiree** Maybe it's terminal.

**Freder** I've had to start sleeping with my legs curled up.

**Desiree** (*laughs*) Oh for God's sake.

**Freder** It hurts less [*that way*].

**Desiree** You ought to get married.

**Freder** Marie – please would you marry me.

**Marie** (*laughs*) Idiot.

**Desiree** He's making you a serious proposal.

**Freder** Extremely serious. We'd make the ideal couple.

**Desiree** She'll think about it. She's begun to appreciate you.

**Freder** I intend to reform.

**Desiree** He intends to reform.

**Freder** More water, please.

**Desiree** Come on – give him an answer.

**Freder** (*gets up*) When the right moment comes, one should consciously embrace bourgeois existence.

**Desiree** Well said. He absolutely means it.

*Marie looks at her.*

His liver's brought him to his senses. Seriously.

**Freder** (*bends over*) I'm in pain.

**Desiree** Don't look at me like that, Marion.

**Alt** What does pain mean? (*He stretches out.*)

**Freder** (*to Marie*) Think about it.

**Marie** Leave me alone.

**Freder** I want to be looked after. I don't like work. Whereas you do like work. We're complementary. And since we've been on first-name terms for three days now, marriage is a mere formality.

**Desiree** Freder's a great believer in the social conventions.

**Freder** I swear that the moment you say yes I'll end my relationship with Lucy.

**Desiree** Still have a relationship, do you?

**Freder** She's exceeding all my expectations.

**Marie** Then marry Lucy.

**Freder** I'm not a pimp.

**Desiree** You're missing the point.

**Marie** Is this your idea of a joke?

**Desiree** Bourgeois existence or suicide. There are no other choices. It's not remotely a joke.

**Freder** (*to Marie*) We have already kissed.

**Marie** (*laughs*) The two of you are totally insane.

**Freder** Do you deny it?

**Desiree** When did you kiss?

**Freder** Yesterday evening.

**Marie** You were there.

**Desiree** I don't remember.

**Marie** You were the one made us.

**Desiree** Rubbish.

**Marie** You were going on and on, Dizzy – you made me kiss him.

**Desiree** I've totally forgotten.

**Marie** That's what happens when you drink.

**Freder** Every breath's like someone's stabbing me. Christ in heaven.

**Desiree** Not so loud. Alt's asleep.

**Alt** Pain's not about actual tissue damage. The bullet-riddled soldier feels nothing and goes on running.

**Desiree** If someone so much as treads on my little toe I reach for my revolver.

**Alt** And if tuberculosis is eating away your lungs you don't even notice. Pain's a thing in itself.

**Marie** I've often trodden on your foot.

**Desiree** I don't dance with you any more.

**Marie** (*laughs*) She's had enough of me.

**Desiree** Freder's waiting for an answer.

**Alt** Stimulus – then mental event – then autosuggestion with the added refinement of an occasional scream. [*Is Alt's definition of pain.*]

**Freder** I need to put my feet in hot water. (*He goes.*)

**Marie** (*softly*) Have you had enough of me?

*Desiree is silent.*

Just say.

**Alt** There are two poles – pain and sleep – to the world of our sensations. We love them both. And both – even total oblivion – are part of life's meaning.

**Desiree** I know a great trick to bring the two poles together.

*Alt looks at her.*

Simultaneous pain and sleep. Do go on, Alt. More tea please.

*Marie pours her tea.*

And more sugar please and cognac [*in the tea*]. (*To Alt.*) Don't overtax your brain.

**Alt** I don't need to overtax my brain.

**Desiree** So you've guessed?

**Marie** Guessed what?

**Desiree** Nothing, gorgeous. You concentrate on your poet.

**Marie** Him?

**Desiree** If you don't make a move soon, they'll end up getting married.

**Marie** That's fine by me.

**Desiree** He'll be faithful unto death. She'll still be laying down the law like a man even when she's an old granny. Don't waste any time, Marion.

**Marie** Are you trying to get rid of me?

**Desiree** You're wonderfully devoted, but I'm just trying to sort your life out.

**Marie** I'm quite capable of doing that without you.

**Desiree** So what about Freder's proposal?

**Marie** (*hugs her*) Why've you started teasing me like this?

**Desiree** (*frees herself*) Stop it.

**Marie** Promise it's just a phase.

**Desiree** She acts like we're married. Some women can't exist outside of a marriage – even if it's to another woman.

**Marie** You're being horrid today.

**Desiree** Now I can see why Dolly couldn't stand it.

**Marie** (*softly*) Hey.

**Desiree** It's unbearable. You've got to stop doing it.

**Marie** Won't you kiss me?

**Desiree** No, I will not kiss you. Go and sit down.

*Marie sits.*

**Desiree** She reminds me of this Hamburg industrialist who was desperate to marry me. Really attractive boy. But kiss him and he nearly had a heart attack. Even when he spent the night with a prostitute it was like they were married. He'd tell her about his mother, about the business, and all about the prospects for 'normalising the political situation in Germany'.

**Marie** I'm getting a grey Mouliné suit made – grey like a man's.

**Desiree** Tomorrow you've got a fitting for the jacket.

**Marie** Tomorrow afternoon.

**Desiree** I'm coming with you. He mustn't cut the waistcoat too low.

**Marie** You can show him.

**Alt** Where did you get your pyjamas? You both look so charming.

**Desiree** Especially Marion. (*Tenderly.*) She's delicious in blue. I chose that blue myself. It goes so well with your hair.

*Kisses her.*

**Marie** Now we're friends again.

**Desiree** Do we have to have a running commentary?

**Marie** I'm sorry?

**Desiree** It's terrifying.

**Marie** What's terrifying?

**Desiree** Commenting on everything. Playing the same old scenes. Like being married. The whole thing's suffocating.

**Alt** Just what is it 's wrong with you?

**Desiree** Spare me – please [*i.e. keep out of it*].

**Alt** I'll stick my finger down your throat.

**Desiree** Thank you.

**Alt** Everyone needs an opportunity to visit the emotional toilet.

**Desiree** And now it's my turn, is it?

**Alt** (*hard*) It's wrong to desert.

**Desiree** You think I care about your moral principles?

**Alt** It's not a moral principle. It's our one social duty towards other human beings.

**Desiree** Now you're getting sentimental.

**Alt** You can do to yourself whatever you like. But the existential prerequisite – the only argument against existential futility – is to live life through to the end. Kill another human being – fine. But kill yourself and you endanger the lives of everyone.

**Desiree** That's the first time I've heard you spout clichés.

**Marie** It's not a cliché. It's the only god-like thing about us.

**Alt** Fine – take your cocaine, or whatever.

**Desiree** This is something we don't agree about. Freder understands me.

**Alt** Freder would never harm himself.

**Desiree** He's happy with life. But he wouldn't stop other people. Not cocaine – barbiturates – a nice big dose of Veronal.* You drift slowly off to sleep – drop deeper and deeper down . . . And at last it's all over.

**Marie** I'm still a complete stranger in other words.

**Desiree** Poor baby.

---

* The first commercial barbiturate brand, marketed by Bayer.

**Marie** You could only think that way if you had no interest in other people.

**Desiree** (*tenderly*) Don't be sad, Marion.

**Marie** (*smiles*) It's the running commentary again.

**Desiree** Don't be sad.

**Marie** I'm still a complete stranger.

**Desiree** Don't we spend our whole lives being strangers?

**Marie** You're not a stranger to me.

**Desiree** We've different characters: to you, nobody's a stranger – to me, it's everyone.
We did try, sweetheart.

**Alt** You didn't try hard enough.

**Desiree** (*smiles*) How hard's hard enough? She's not the one. I didn't need to sleep with her for eight nights to work that out.

**Marie** (*softly*) You take the magic out of everything.

**Desiree** Perhaps. But doesn't magic imply resistance in the first place?
You're not the one, Marion.

**Marie** (*nods*) I'm not the one.

**Desiree** That first night I lifted you off this floor and onto my bed, it really felt like you were mine. But it wasn't me you made love to, it was your own pain.

**Marie** Please don't.

**Desiree** She's embarrassed. Alt's not a man, Alt's just a half-baked woman, you could strip off in front of him. Even the next day I found the two of us a bit bizarre.

**Marie** Please please don't.

**Desiree** I was really patient with you. I'd never 've been so patient with a man.

**Marie** I can't help how I'm made.

**Desiree** Poor little foolish girl.

**Marie** When I was small I played with dolls, not swords and hobby horses.

**Desiree** (*hugs Marie's knees*) My poor poor innocent love.

**Marie** (*softly*) You can't ask me to be a man.

**Desiree** Are you unhappy?

**Marie** (*softly*) Yes.

**Desiree** And find me disappointing too.

**Marie** Yes.

**Desiree** (*kisses her*) Pitiful, aren't we.

*They hug each other. Pause.*

What's going to happen to us? Two years from now I'll be a doctor. I'll be like you. Is that the dream?

**Marie** I don't have dreams any more.

**Desiree** Junior doctor in the general hospital. The smell of iodine and carbolic. That stench for life.

**Marie** It used to seem like music.

**Desiree** Your whole life in disgusting charitable contact with total strangers – with the unwashed.

**Marie** It used to seem like music that would soothe the pain of thousands.

**Desiree** I've never believed in my fellow man. It's absurd to sacrifice yourself for others. Even when you *are* soothing their pain, they'd rather be alone.

88

## SCENE TWO

*Lucy, strikingly dressed.*

**Lucy** (*slightly drunk*) Is there anything else the young ladies or the gentleman need?

**Desiree** What *are* you wearing?

**Lucy** Is there anything else the ladies or the gentleman may need?

**Marie** Are you going out?

**Lucy** (*nods*) I have to.

**Desiree** Alone?

**Lucy** (*smiles*) Oh, I'm never alone for long.

**Desiree** So who is it keeps you company?

**Lucy** I don't care – whoever.

**Desiree** Come and sit with us.

**Lucy** It'll make me late.

**Desiree** But we're all feeling sad. Cheer us up.

**Lucy** I'm never sad.

**Desiree** You're such a happy little thing.

**Lucy** I love it, I love it, I love my life.

**Desiree** That's such a gorgeous voice you've got.

**Lucy** (*suddenly*) I'm coming straight back. (*Goes.*)

**Desiree** Poor little thing. I'm so envious.

**Marie** How does he do it?

**Alt** Freder?

**Marie** (*nods*) No need to think for yourself any more. No more will of your own – everything's taken care of – like being anaesthetised.

**Desiree** You'd never go on the game.

**Marie** But imagine never having to think.

**Desiree** I could do what she's doing: no anaesthetic – no Freder – just me.

## SCENE THREE

*Lucy with wine and glasses.*

**Desiree** We've already got brandy.

**Lucy** This is good wine.

**Alt** Where did you get wine from?

**Lucy** There's another bottle if you want.

**Desiree** I could kiss you.

**Lucy** Let's all drink a toast.

**Marie** To the two girls from Passau.

**Lucy** (*laughs*) I'd forgotten about Passau.

**Marie** What about your fiancé?

**Lucy** My fiancé?

**Desiree** She's got a fiancé?

**Marie** In Passau.

**Desiree** She's got a fiancé in Passau.

**Lucy** The young lady's welcome to make fun of me.

**Desiree** Please: call me Desiree.

**Lucy** (*laughs*) I don't hate you any more.

**Desiree** (*surprised*) You hated me?

**Lucy** A lot.

**Desiree** Why?

*Lucy is silent.*

**Marie** I feel so miserable.

**Alt** Come over here and relax.

**Desiree** But not any more?

**Lucy** Don't be angry. The young lady's so beautiful.

**Desiree** Please: call me Desiree.

**Lucy** I don't understand Herr Freder.

**Desiree** Don't understand him how?

**Lucy** Why he doesn't love you any more.

**Desiree** But you're pleased.

**Lucy** I'm over the moon.

**Desiree** D'you love him that much?

**Lucy** That much and more.

**Desiree** That's beautiful – kiss me. (*Hugs her.*)

**Alt** For all her world-weariness she's still just a child.

**Lucy** Now all we need's some music. We can just sit and listen.

**Desiree** (*winds up the gramophone*) Let's dance.

**Lucy** But the gentleman doesn't dance.

**Desiree** When's Freder collecting you?

**Lucy** I go on my own. He trusts me.

**Desiree** Does he take your money?

**Lucy** Not a penny. Even though I owe him everything.

**Desiree** D'you earn a lot? Tell me.

**Lucy** Every day's different.

**Desiree** Tell me.

**Lucy** Someone's even proposed.

**Desiree** There's no way you'd accept.

**Lucy** He's not got a chance in hell.

**Desiree** You should get yourself a little flat.

**Lucy** (*quickly*) No.

**Desiree** Frau Schimmelbrot will catch you.

**Lucy** I'm not scared of her.

**Desiree** I see. Because Freder's living here.

**Lucy** (*quickly*) Shh.

**Desiree** I won't give you away if you tell me everything. Who let you have the coat and the make-up that first evening, mmm?

**Lucy** (*laughs*) I was so scared!

**Desiree** But it all went very smoothly, yes?

**Lucy** It all went very quickly.

**Desiree** Tell me.

**Lucy** It's all much simpler than you'd expect.

**Desiree** D'you get many?

**Lucy** I don't really count.

**Desiree** Come on – I want details. How old are you?

**Lucy** Eighteen.

**Desiree** Very good.
And you go with anyone?

**Lucy** Yes.

**Desiree** You don't care what they look like?

**Lucy** I don't pay much attention.

**Desiree** Excellent. You do realise what might happen?

**Lucy** You can't get babies doing that.

**Desiree** Why can't you get babies doing that?

**Lucy** Herr Freder said so.

**Desiree** How much money do you get?

**Lucy** Yesterday I slipped out this one's wallet while he was asleep. I wanted to find out who he was.

**Desiree** Fantastic. Who was he?

**Lucy** (*laughs*) A boxer.

**Desiree** (*suddenly*) I'll come with you for a bit.

**Lucy** (*anxious*) No one will talk to me.

**Desiree** I'll do my face like yours.

**Lucy** No no – not both together.

**Desiree** Don't look so worried – some men like two at a time.

**Lucy** I don't know about that.

**Desiree** There's lots of things you don't know about. Wait here, Lucy. I'll get myself ready.

**Marie** Are you going to change?

**Desiree** (*laughs*) I'm going with her.

**Marie**  You must be mad.

**Desiree**  What's the point of being sane?

**Alt**  You come with me, Lucy. [*He wants to get her out.*]

**Desiree**  (*laughs*) Don't think you're going to stop me.

**Marie**  You're in for a fight then.

**Desiree**  I'm going on the game.

**Marie**  Dizzy – don't say that.

**Desiree**  (*imitates her*) 'Dizzy – don't say that.' I'm going on the game.

*Goes into her room.*

**Lucy**  (*surprised*) On the game?

**Alt**  Come on.

**Lucy**  I'm not on the game.

**Alt**  Of course you're not.

**Lucy**  I'm not going to be insulted.

**Alt**  Well said.

**Lucy**  Herr Freder will teach her a lesson.

**Alt**  Yes you complain to him.

**Lucy**  She's the one got dumped.

*Marie goes into Desiree's room.*

**Alt**  That's what she can't accept. Now hurry up and come.

**Lucy**  But you must please leave me at the corner, won't you?

**Alt**  Of course I will.

*Both go.*

## SCENE FOUR

**Marie** (*in adjacent room*) Stop being stupid.

**Desiree** (*in adjacent room*) Give me the key.*

**Marie** (*in adjacent room*) I refuse to let you [*go out as a whore*].

**Desiree** (*comes in and runs to Marie's entrance door*) I'll do what the hell I like.

**Marie** (*goes after her, blocks the door*) No.

**Desiree** You won't let me out?

**Marie** Dizzy.

**Desiree** I'll hurt you.

**Marie** Fine – hurt me.

**Desiree** You're not my mother.

**Marie** I'm not your mother.

*Desiree attacks her. Marie pushes her away.*

**Marie** You'll have to kill me first.

**Desiree** (*furious*) I wouldn't give you the satisfaction.

**Marie** Dizzy.

**Desiree** I want to go out on the street.

**Marie** I know.

**Desiree** You have no right.

**Marie** I have no right.

**Desiree** You're the mad one, not me.

* The key to the unseen other entrance to Desiree's room.

**Marie** I'm the mad one, not you.

**Desiree** Let me out. I'm not sleeping with you ever again.

**Marie** We'll sleep separately. I'll go to bed in here.

**Desiree** You bore me. You disgust me.

**Marie** You're the one wanted me.

**Desiree** And now what I want is a man – a stranger stinking of sweat – a boxer like *she* had. Let me out on the street. Or are you jealous?

**Marie** Maybe I am jealous.

**Desiree** You can't think straight any more.

**Marie** Maybe I can't think straight / any more.

**Desiree** It's like having a fucking husband.

*Pause.*

**Marie** (*tenderly*) Dizzy.

*Desiree is silent.*

(*Sits beside her.*) My poor crazy sweetheart.

**Desiree** Give me my key.

**Marie** No.

*Desiree goes into her room. Marie stays sitting,
exhausted. Begins to drink. Goes into Desiree's room.*

**Desiree** (*in adjacent room*) Leave me alone.

**Marie** (*in adjacent room*) I *am* leaving you alone.

**Desiree** (*in adjacent room*) Give me my key back.

*Marie laughs, comes back in with blanket and pillow.
Makes up a bed on the chaise longue. She drinks more.*

*Alt.*

**Marie** She's in her room.

**Alt** Any calmer?

**Marie** The opposite.

**Alt** We'll calm her down tomorrow.

**Marie** Want another glass?

**Alt** No thanks.
  Goodnight.

**Marie** Alt.

**Alt** Yes?

**Marie** (*pause*) How far did you walk with Lucy?

**Alt** She ran off the moment we got downstairs.

**Marie** She's very attractive.
  Alt.

**Alt** Yes?

**Marie** (*pause*) Goodnight.

**Alt** What is it?

**Marie** I shouldn't've stopped her.

**Alt** Rubbish.

**Marie** I'll tell her she can go if she wants.

**Alt** Just leave her. She'll sleep it off.

**Marie** She won't sleep at all tonight.

**Alt** Leave her to think.

**Marie**  She loves playing the victim.

**Alt**  It keeps her alive.

**Marie**  (*pause*) You don't desert.

**Alt**  (*firm*) YOU DON'T DESERT.

**Marie**  Don't shout at me like that.

**Alt**  (*suddenly*) I think I'll sleep here tonight.

　　*Marie laughs.*

I'm suspicious.

**Marie**  Don't you trust me?

**Alt**  Even less than her.

**Marie**  (*amazed*) What?

**Alt**  She's used to dealing with depression.

**Marie**  And I'm not.

**Alt**  And you're not. She's very used to being disappointed.

**Marie**  And I'm not.

**Alt**  And you're not.

**Marie**  You always talk about *her*.

**Alt**  As for you –

**Marie**  Yes?

**Alt**  Your mind's too crowded. You need to let go.

**Marie**  So what are your words of wisdom?

**Alt**  Take life less seriously. Forget who you are.
Rediscover yourself. And do evil unto others.

**Marie**  Amen.

**Alt** I lay down the law – it's what men do.

**Marie** Keep your ten commandments to yourself.

**Alt** Fall in love with her again. Ask her forgiveness.

**Marie** (*looks at him*) I'll ask her forgiveness.

**Alt** Henceforward you're her slave.

**Marie** (*laughs*) Perhaps.

**Alt** She'll treat you very badly.

**Marie** She already treats me very badly. Don't worry.

**Alt** Your choice.

**Marie** You go to sleep now. Anyway, Freder's around.

**Alt** I wouldn't rely on Freder.

**Marie** We don't need supervision.

**Alt** Goodnight.

**Marie** (*quick*) Alt.

**Alt** Yes?

**Marie** (*pause*) Goodnight.

*Alt goes.*

(*At Desiree's door.*) Open up, you silly baby. – Are you already in bed? – Here's your key. I won't stop you. If it's something you have to do, then do it. – Talk to me. I'm leaving the key just here [*on floor*]. You only need to open it a crack. (*Pause. Softly.*) Forgive me, Dizzy. (*Goes on her knees.*) Forgive me, Dizzy. I was worried about you. Talk to me! (*Angry.*) Aren't I even worth talking to? (*Hammers on the door with her fists.*) I won't go away. I'll spend the whole night here if you don't open this door.

## SCENE SIX

*Desiree in nightdress opens the door.*

**Desiree** (*sinks into Marie's arms*) Kiss me.

**Marie** My love.

*Kisses her.*

**Desiree** (*very tender*) Forgive me, Marion.

**Marie** My love.

*They sit close together on the bed.*

**Desiree** (*smiling*) Let's die together.

**Marie** No.

**Desiree** Help me, Marion.

**Marie** (*cries*) No.

**Desiree** I can't not, little sister. I feel anaesthetised. Like the mask's over my face. I'm touching you through fog.

**Marie** I'll carry you to bed.

**Desiree** It would be such a tiny step.

**Marie** Don't say that.

**Desiree** I'm already halfway there. Just one more tiny step. Do it, Marie. Put Veronal in my glass.

**Marie** (*pleads*) Please stop talking about it.

*Pause.*

**Desiree** (*kisses her*) I was dreaming you'd help me.

**Marie** No more now.

**Desiree** Then you called me – banged on the door and woke me up. Tell me you'll do it. Say yes, even if it isn't true.

**Marie** Why d'you have to torture me?

**Desiree** Just say yes. Humour me.

**Marie** (*softly*) Yes.

**Desiree** Thank you.

**Marie** Now I'm carrying you to bed.

**Desiree** Look into my eyes.

**Marie** (*takes hold of her*) Come on.

**Desiree** Strong beautiful eyes.

**Marie** (*carrying her across the room*) You're going to have a lovely sleep.

**Desiree** You're beautiful, Marion.

*Suddenly hugs her.*

Forgive me.

**Marie** I'll sit with you till you've gone to sleep.

*Carries her out.*

**Marie** (*from adjoining room*) Comfy now?

**Desiree** (*from adjoining room*) I love you, Marion.

**Marie** (*from adjoining room*) I'm turning the light out.

*Adjoining room goes dark.*

Go to sleep, sweetheart.

**Desiree** (*from adjoining room, very softly*) I love you.

**Marie** (*after slight pause*) Are you asleep?

*No answer.*

*Freder, without jacket.*

**Freder** (*goes over to Desiree's open door*) You two aren't asleep in there, are you?

**Marie** (*comes in and shuts the door*) She is.

**Freder** And you're tired too?

**Marie** Yes.

**Freder** So early? (*Pours wine.*)

**Marie** You're not supposed to be drinking.

**Freder** We're not married yet.

**Marie** Don't joke.

**Freder** What makes you think it's a joke?

**Marie** You're mixing me up with Lucy.

**Freder** Lucy's an amazing little thing.

**Marie** So I've seen.

**Freder** She sleepwalks through life and never looks back. I envy her.

**Marie** How could you make somebody do that?

**Freder** Make her? She volunteers.

**Marie** You know exactly what I mean.

**Freder** I've never seen you looking so beautiful.

**Marie** You're not supposed to be drinking.

**Freder** One more glass makes no difference. That footbath's worked miracles. I'm ready for anything.

**Marie** Leave me alone.

**Freder** It's too early for me to sleep.

**Marie** Well I'm tired.

**Freder** You're not being much of a hostess.

**Marie** (*exhausted*) Please don't do this.

**Freder** I've never seen you looking so beautiful.

**Marie** I can hardly stand up.

**Freder** You're so pale it could drive a man insane.

**Marie** I feel miserable.

**Freder** So do I.

**Marie** I'm anxious about Dizzy.

**Freder** What's wrong with Dizzy?

**Marie** She wanted to go on the street. I stopped her. I shouldn't've done.

**Freder** That's not for Dizzy. Dizzy's like putty – but with a will of steel. The world's most unfortunate combination.

**Marie** You're the one made her lose her bearings.

**Freder** She ran away at seventeen. I've simply speeded up the inevitable.

**Marie** I wish she'd never met you.

**Freder** (*laughs*) You all need me to live.

**Marie** You are totally deranged.

**Freder** You know you want me.

**Marie** That is so ludicrous.

**Freder** You want me like you want the knife.

*Approaches her.*

**Marie**  Off me.

**Freder**  You can smell blood. There's only one way out: marry me.

**Marie**  (*laughs*) Funny way out.

**Freder**  Opt for bourgeois existence and avoid catastrophe.

**Marie**  You sound like Desiree.

**Freder**  Or I could put you on the game – like Lucy.

**Marie**  (*looks up*) You're joking.

**Freder**  You're like a wind-up toy – you just need to be put on the right track – doesn't matter which. You could do insane twenty-hour shifts in theatre. You could be mother of ten children. You could be toughest whore on the block. You contain all possibilities. You are the ultimate cliché of a young woman's incredible potential.

**Marie**  Thank you for the options.

**Freder**  But what you cannot be, is nothing. That would destroy you.

**Marie**  You can't upset me.

**Freder**  I want to help.

**Marie**  Help your friend Lucy.

**Freder**  She doesn't need me any more. Lucy just needed waking up.

**Marie**  Well, I don't.

**Freder**  That just isn't true.

**Marie**  Says who?

**Freder** I'm not stupid. You want waking up. While you had Dolly, you were still comatose.

**Marie** Leave him out of it.

**Freder** Now it's just you: you feel more alert – yes. But wake up too late and you're dead.

**Marie** Will you please please leave me alone?

**Freder** I repeat my offer – in all seriousness.

**Marie** I'm already married.

**Freder** To Dizzy?

**Marie** To Dizzy.

**Freder** You'll soon be a widow.

**Marie** (*jumps up*) Bastard.

**Freder** At last –

**Marie** I hate you.

**Freder** – a declaration of love.

**Marie** I could kill you.

**Freder** Excellent. The sea! The sea!

**Marie** (*wild*) I'm not falling into your trap.

**Freder** Are you quite sure?

**Marie** You don't know me.

**Freder** I've still got you.

**Marie** You wouldn't dare.

**Freder** I'm not even touching you but I've still got you.

**Marie** In your dreams.

**Freder** It's your dream too.

**Marie** I'd rather kill myself.

**Freder** Am I really so repellent?

**Marie** You're a bastard.

**Freder** So you said.

**Marie** I hate you.

**Freder** Good.

**Marie** Just get out of my room.

**Freder** Angry suits you – makes your face burn.

**Marie** If you won't go, I'm running out now.

**Freder** Try it.

**Marie** I won't be responsible for my actions.

**Freder** Perfect.

**Marie** (*runs to the door*) I can't stand this.

**Freder** It's dark out there [*in the lobby*].

**Marie** I'll go to Frau Schimmelbrot.

**Freder** She won't like that.

**Marie** (*erupts*) JUST LEAVE ME ALONE.

**Freder** Trapped.

**Marie** Shut up or I'll strangle you.

**Freder** What is it I've said?

**Marie** What if I beg you –

**Freder** Down on your knees.

**Marie** – will you leave me alone?

**Freder** Down on your knees.

**Marie** (*goes down on her knees*) Leave me alone – I'm begging you.

**Freder**  And say the Our Father.

**Marie**  Jesus Christ I'm going mad.

**Freder**  Our Father, which art / in heaven.

**Marie**  I can't stand this.

**Freder**  Give us this day our / daily bread –

**Marie**  (*attacks Freder*) Get out.

**Freder**  (*holds her*) And forgive us our trespasses –

**Marie**  Get out.

**Freder**  As we forgive those –

*Kisses her.*

You've never been so beautiful.

**Marie**  (*tries to get free*) I'll strangle you.

**Freder**  Angry means hot.

**Marie**  Get off.

**Freder**  (*kisses her*) After the Our Father we can die in peace.

**Marie**  I'll scream.

*They fall on the bed. Marie manages to struggle free and runs into Desiree's room.*

**Freder**  (*goes after her*) That's not going to help you.

*Goes into Desiree's room. Pause. Marie comes back in and sinks into a chair. After a while Freder appears at the door.*

Too late.

**Marie**  What do we do with her?

**Freder**  Nothing.

**Marie**  We should get Alt.

**Freder**  Too late.

*Pause.*

**Marie**  We should still call a doctor.

**Freder**  She's dead.

*Pause.*

**Marie**  I tried to get in but the door was locked. I had to hammer on it before she heard me.

**Freder**  She was already halfway there.

**Marie**  How could it be so quick?

**Freder**  Depends on the amount.

**Marie**  But how did she get so much?

**Freder**  (*simply*) I got it for her.

**Marie**  (*softly*) You terrify me.

**Freder**  You want me to leave the room?

**Marie**  (*quickly*) No.

**Freder**  You wanted to be alone.

**Marie**  (*softly*) Murderer.

*Freder is silent.*

Why did you do it?

**Freder**  She'd've drowned herself otherwise.

*Pause.*

**Marie**  What do we do?

**Freder**  She asked me for it.

**Marie**  Murderer.

**Freder**  Means nothing.

**Marie**  Poor little sparrow, my poor little sister.

**Freder**  I'll leave you alone.

**Marie**  You'll stay just where you are.

**Freder**  Then promise me no speeches.

**Marie**  We'll both not talk.

*Pause. Freder drinks.*

**Marie**  (*softly*) Some for me. (*Pause.*) Now you've got me where you wanted me.

**Freder**  Got you where?

**Marie**  Don't pretend.

**Freder**  You're talking rubbish.

**Marie**  Drink. (*Points at Desiree's door.*) Is that door properly closed?

**Freder**  Does it bother you?

**Marie**  Drink.

**Freder**  She's not very likely to hear us.

**Marie**  (*goes to door*) It's shut.

**Freder**  You want to go to sleep?

**Marie**  What do *you* think?

**Freder**  I don't think anything.

**Marie**  I'll whisper it in your ear.

**Freder** (*dodges her*) You don't need to whisper –

**Marie** Don't run away from me.

**Freder** – just say it.

**Marie** (*chases him*) Are you afraid of me?

**Freder** I don't understand you.

**Marie** Frightened I'll bite your ear off?

**Freder** (*catches her*) You're delirious.

**Marie** Maybe.

**Freder** It's better I go. We should fetch a doctor.

**Marie** Down on your knees.

**Freder** Goodnight.

**Marie** I said down on your knees.

**Freder** Marie.

**Marie** You'll get more from me than an Our Father.

**Freder** What is it you want?

**Marie** Pretty please and Doggie will get a nice sweetie – say pretty pretty please.

**Freder** You're being strange.

**Marie** I'm being beautiful.

**Freder** Marie.

**Marie** I have never been so beautiful.

**Freder** Stop.

**Marie** I've not forgotten what you said.

**Freder** There's a dead woman in that room.

**Marie**  You think I care?

**Freder**  There's a dead woman in that room.

**Marie**  Means nothing. Drink. (*She drinks.*)

**Freder**  You've lost control.

**Marie**  Makes me more attractive: want me, you can have me.

**Freder**  Don't play games with me.

**Marie**  The sea! The sea!

**Freder**  (*incensed*) I said don't play games.

    *Chases her.*

**Marie**  (*laughs*) Catch me.

    *Chase.*

Catch me. Bastard. I hate you.

**Freder**  (*catches her*) Stop this now.

**Marie**  (*laughs hysterically*) Drink – come on.

**Freder**  I'm warning you.

**Marie**  You're still not drunk enough.

**Freder**  (*at the door*) Before I go completely insane –

**Marie**  It's dark out there [*in the lobby*].

**Freder**  I'll find the way.

**Marie**  You'll knock over a chair.

**Freder**  Won't be the end of the world.

**Marie**  Frau Schimmelbrot won't like it.

**Freder**  *This* is the end of the world.

**Marie**  Means nothing.

**Freder**  JUST LEAVE ME ALONE.

**Marie**  Trapped. (*Tears open her top.*) I'm going to bed.

**Freder**  Marie.

**Marie**  (*laughing*) I hate you. I despise you. D'you give up?

**Freder**  I won't be responsible for / what happens.

**Marie**  Our Father who art / in heaven –

**Freder**  (*incensed*) SHUT THE FUCK UP.

**Marie**  Forgive us our trespasses –

*Freder throws himself at her.*

(*Constantly laughing.*) Is that the best you can do? Even Dolly can do that. (*Wriggles free.*) As we forgive them / who trespass –

**Freder**  (*chases her*) You wait.

**Marie**  Well come on: I'm waiting.

**Freder**  Dear God.

*Catches her.*

**Marie**  Who's God? – Means nothing. (*Wriggles free.*) You're tearing my lovely pyjamas. Come on Dolly – you can do it!

**Freder**  (*beside himself*) I am not your Dolly. My shoe's come off.

**Marie**  Run, Dolly – run run run.

**Freder**  No – no more running.

**Marie**  Dolly can kiss too. And much more sweetly.

(*Wriggles free.*) You're hurting me. He can bite too. In the neck, Dolly.

**Freder** I am not your Dolly.

**Marie** You're knocking the table over.

*Freder throws her onto the bed.*

First another drink. You need lots lots more to drink.

**Freder** I'm not drinking any more.

**Marie** Put out the light.

*Tries to get free.*

**Freder** (*beside himself*) KEEP STILL.

**Marie** I like you. You're strong. Put out the light.

*Runs away.*

**Freder** To hell with the light. Keep still.

*Marie puts out the light; it's dark.*

**Marie** Do it – do it – do it.

**Freder** Don't try and escape.

**Marie** I'll never escape. You're too strong. Do it.

**Freder** Marie.

**Marie** (*from deep in her soul*) Do it. Kill me.

*Curtain.*

## VARIANT ENDING

*From page 109:*

**Marie** What do we do?

**Freder** She asked me for it.

**Marie** Murderer.

**Freder** Means nothing.

**Marie** Poor little sparrow, my poor little sister.

**Freder** I'll leave you alone.

**Marie** You'll stay just where you are.

**Freder** Then promise me no speeches.

**Marie** Let's both not talk.

*Pause. Freder drinks.*

My little sister.

**Freder** We should call a doctor – you're right.

**Marie** (*quickly*) Don't go.

**Freder** But if I frighten you –

**Marie** I'm more frightened of being alone.

**Freder** More frightened than you are of me – really?

**Marie** Just drink.

*Freder comes to the table, drinks.*

(*Softly.*) Some for me.

*Freder pours her a drink.*

(*Empty.*) What's going to happen to me?

**Freder** If you can ask the question, you already know the answer.

*Marie looks at him.*

And the answer is: one way or another, life goes on.

**Marie** Life goes on.

**Freder** When the moment arrives, one should embrace bourgeois existence – quite consciously.

**Marie** I'm thinking about her dead.

**Freder** You're fated to be bourgeois. Suicide's not you – you simply couldn't do it.

**Marie** (*nods*) I couldn't do it.

**Freder** All those times recently you've thought about it, yes? – but found it impossible.

**Marie** Completely impossible.

**Freder** To everyone's astonishment we find that even this fine specimen has her limits. I want to be looked after and have, as you know, a limitless aversion to work. You, on the other hand, love work. Thus making us the ideal couple.

*Marie looks at him in despair.*

No alternative.

*He sits at the table and begins to eat.*

**Marie** (*softly*) Help me.

**Freder** (*with his mouth full*) You all come to me in the end, one way or another. I've said that before – but some things have to be said over and over before they actually happen. None of you can live without me. If no one takes control you're all of you lost.

**Marie** Help me.

**Freder** Eat. Life goes on.

*Marie starts to sob.*

I said eat.

*Marie, in tears, reaches for the food.*
*The End.*